Jonathan Goodma ⌷⌷⌷ some years a theatre director and ⌷⌷⌷ producer. As well as being the author of a number of books on crime, he is editor of five previous anthologies of classic true murder stories published by Sphere Books. In addition he has written several novels and a volume of poetry and recently edited *The Master Eccentric*, the journals of his fellow crime historian and writer Rayner Heppenstall. Jonathan Goodman is a member of the British Academy of Forensic Sciences, the Medico-Legal Society and Our Society.

THE VINTAGE
CAR MURDERS

Edited by
Jonathan Goodman

SPHERE BOOK LIMITED

For Jack Hammond –
whose idea it was.

A SPHERE BOOK

First published in Great Britain by W. H. Allen & Co. Plc 1988
Published by Sphere Books Ltd 1990

Copyright © Jonathan Goodman 1988

Printed and bound in Great Britain by
Richard Clay Ltd, Bungay, Suffolk

ISBN 0 7474 0480 1

Sphere Books Ltd
A Division of
Macdonald & Co (Publishers) Ltd
27 Wrights Lane, London W8 5TZ
A member of Maxwell Pergamon Publishing Corporation plc

Contents

Jonathan Goodman
A Wagonload of Murderers   1

Jonathan Goodman
The Four-Wheeled Crematorium   5

Richard Whittington-Egan
Fire-lit Tales of Murder   37

Albert Borowitz
The Judge's Black Cadillac   58

Ian Forbes
Woman of Evil   66

Thomas M. McDade
Looking for Baby-Face   96

Bill Knox
The Hit-and-Run Murderer   105

Two Single-Horsepower Cases:

     The Reverend Evelyn Burnaby
     The Hansom Hearse   117

     Edmund Pearson
     The Wicked Hansom   127

The Hon. H. Fletcher Moulton
The Case of the Equivocal Cabbie   132

CONTENTS

Joseph Gollomb
Nemesis in Texas   174

Bernard O'Donnell
Killed After a Cuddle   187

Albert Borowitz
A Murder in Camelot   196

Jonathan Goodman
Last Stop, Arcadia   211

Acknowledgments and Sources   218

A Wagonload of Murderers

PUBLISHERS DON'T LIKE hyphens in titles. If that were not so, this book would be called "The Vintage Car-Murders", and I should not need to explain that the adjective describes a collection of murder cases in which comfy road-vehicles of different eras and various mileages were accessory to, part-motives for, or simply scenes of the crimes. And I should not have needed to find out what distinguishes a vintage vehicle from other elderly ones. This is what I learnt:

The Veteran Car Club accepts vehicles built by the end of 1918, regarding pre-1904 machines as *true* veterans, and (extending our last conscientious King Edward's "ianism" nearly nine years past his reign) calling the rest Edwardian. The vintage period comes next, lasting, without argument, till the end of the Twenties – coincidentally, about the same dozen years that are generally acclaimed as the Golden Age of English Murders. Some extraordinarily elegant or powerful cars that were made between 1930 and, roughly speaking, the end of the war are known as vintage thoroughbreds. Some distinctive post-war cars are called classics.

There.

I had plenty of cases to choose from. I would have had more if, when compiling earlier volumes of this series, I had foreseen this one and put aside cases that fitted it: the "stock" would therefore have included the murder of Irene Wilkins by Thomas Allaway, the chauffeur whose mistaken idea of the spelling of Bournemouth, the town where he worked, helped bring about his execution (F. Tennyson Jesse's account of the case, appropriate also to *The Christmas Murders*, actually appears in the first of these books, *The Pleasures of Murder*), and, similar to the Allaway case in that it was set off by a small ad, the Southampton Garage Mystery (which is explained in

The Seaside Murders) – and, as I believe that some items in
any anthology should be at the very edge of what the book-
title allows, I might have saved the Brides-in-the-Bath case
(instead of putting it among the *Seaside* ones) on the ground
that George Joseph Smith was, so he scribbled to a prying
parent of a girl he intended to be the legacied widower of,
closely related both to transporters and to persons quaintly
transported:"My mother was a Buss horse, my father a Cab
driver, my sister a rough rider over the arctic regions – my
brothers were all gallant sailors on a steam-roller." (Smith's
claim regarding his maternity reminds me to wonder if anyone
knows how the judges' epitome of reasonableness came to be
sitting on a *Clapham* omnibus – which, judging by statements
from spokespeople for the London Regional Transport
workers' union, is as reckless a thing to do at night nowadays
as to travel by Tube anywhere near Clapham, which is adjacent
to Brixton, whatever the hour.)

Excepting *Pleasures*, which was not expected to have antho-
logical kin, this collection has more US cases than the others
put together. It would have been nice if I had been able to
include an Anglo-American tale: something along Crippen
lines – an American customer of Hertz UK, driven to
murderous distraction by the wife's back-seat driving – or
something reminiscent of the murder in Missouri by the
unsettled Englishman, Hugh Brooks (who, like Crippen a
quarter of a century later, was arrested thousands of nautical
miles from the land of his crime) – the mercy-killing of a
tourist in a room, "en-suite", of a *Psycho*-style motel.

The exemplary Anglo-American car-murder ought to be
here – but, I'm sorry, is not. I am speaking of the "for-fun"
shooting, on the Great West Road out of London on a night
in October 1944, of George Heath, the unlicensed plier for
hire of a grey Ford V8 saloon, by a GI, AWOL, named Karl
Gustav Hulten (but calling himself Ricki Allen), who was
ably assisted – perhaps before the act, certainly immediately
afterwards – by his Welsh floozie, Elizabeth Maud Jones
(alias Georgina Grayson, the name she strip-teased under). Even
before the awful couple were caught, let alone trying to put
the blame on each other, the press called what they had done
The Inky-Fingers Murder (for the simple reason that a few of
the victim's fingers were inky), but that title was almost as soon

supplanted by The Cleft-Chin Case (for the simpler reason that the victim had that facial peculiarity). Both Hulten and Jones were found guilty and sentenced to death, but only he was hanged. She, having been reprieved, spent nine years in prison.

I wish I knew what then became of her. If she isn't dead by now, the summer of 1988, she is sixty-two. It is to be hoped, for other people's sake, that Bernard Shaw was wrong: in a letter of his that *The Times* published on 5 March 1945, though she was still scheduled for execution, he remarked that "her mental condition unfits her to live in a civilized community".

The crime that she helped Hulten with does not deserve a long recounting – but because, for one thing, asides from the necessary evidence at the trial add up to a telling or reminding of how it *felt* to be living in London in the doodlebug months of the war, and for another, the Home Secretary's decision to let the American hang but to save his British confederate must have been taken despite much politicking by members of the Coalition Government who feared a harming of the "special relationship", the case should be expertly examined and chronicled. So far as I have seen, none of the existing accounts is worth reviving. It is a great shame that, at different times while the "Notable British Trials" were being published by Hodge of Edinburgh, poor-imitation series came from other publishers, each of those series occasionally including a trial which would otherwise have been presented, far more usefully, as an NBT. Three trials (of William "Lord Haw-Haw" Joyce; of Thomas Ley, once the Minister of Justice in his native New South Wales, and Lawrence Smith – who, though they would not have got far as murderers without the cars they borrowed from a subsequently-turncoat henchman, I have decided are best held over for some other collection; and of Alfred Arthur Rouse, who comes first herein) appeared as NBTs as well as in one or other of the inferior series, but the trial of Hulten and Jones was among those that the Hodges, Harry and his son Jim, shied away from because of direct commercial competition – for book-publishing was, to them, a just-about-affordable labour of love, a sideline stemming from and often subsidized by their paying trades, as shorthand-writers to the Scottish courts of law and as jobbing printers, considerably for Scottish grocers. The introductory essay in the Hulten/Jones book that pre-empted an NBT was one of the accounts of the case that I considered.

The Hodge trial volumes, War Crimes and all, have recently been republished – not as books, but on microfiche – by the Gregg Publishing Company of Reigate, Surrey. Anyone in his right mind would prefer not to have to twiddle knobs so as to be able to read something, but as – so I am informed – no public or institutional library has all of the proper books (some of the early titles had print-runs of only 250 or so, and most of the titles were out of print when the last of them appeared in 1959), many readers of *this* book will have cause to thank Gregg for microscopic mercies.

The Four-Wheeled Crematorium

Jonathan Goodman

AT TWO O'CLOCK on the morning of Thursday, 6
November 1930, the lane leading from the main London road
to the village of Hardingstone, near Northampton, was
burnished by a full moon. The moonlight, unimpeded by even
a wisp of cloud, prickled on the frosted hedgerows and gave
the rough surface of the lane the look of emery paper.

Two young men, William Bailey and his cousin, Alfred
Brown, were walking to their homes in Hardingstone. They
had been to a Guy Fawkes' Night dance at the Salon ballroom
in Northampton. Tired but happy, unconcerned by the thought
that in a few hours' time they would have to retrace their steps
to the town – William to clock in at Barratt's shoe factory,
Alfred to open the luggage shop in Bridge Street where he
had recently been taken on as a repairer of suitcases – they
turned left into the lane.

Towards the village, the steel-blue of the moonlight was
splashed with a far brighter light. Yellow, red and violet-
coloured flames lanced from a source beyond a slight bend in
the lane. Though quite a spectacle, it was not a surprising one
to the two young men, who had seen any number of bonfires
during the past eight hours or so. Here was another, they
thought – a symbol of celebration that was outlasting most of
its kind.

Hurrying now, not wanting to miss any fun, William and
Alfred approached the fire. But then, with the source of the
leaping flames still out of sight, they experienced the first of
several shocks.

A man emerged from a gap in the hedge on the right-hand
side of the lane.

Only partly because of his fresh professional interest in
luggage, Alfred registered the fact that the man was carrying

an expensive-looking attaché-case. He was wearing, unbuttoned, a belted raincoat – almost white, it looked – over a dark suit. "A city-gent's outfit," Alfred thought.

He shot a glance at his cousin. The expression on William's face showed that he too was perplexed. As for the stranger – well, he appeared not so much confused as frightened out of his wits. He hesitated a moment, his eyes staring, his lips moving but not making words, then scurried past William and Alfred towards the main road. When he had gone about fifteen yards, he shouted in a shaky voice, "It looks as if someone's had a bonfire."

The two young men continued on their way. When they came to the bend in the lane, they looked back. The stranger had reached the road. Apparently uncertain of his direction, he took a few steps to the right, towards Northampton, then turned towards London. The last they saw of him, he was standing aimlessly in the middle of the road.

But now William and Alfred had something else to think about. They were close enough to the fire for their faces to be rouged by the glare – close enough to hear the crackle and splutter of whatever was burning – close enough to be aware of a smell that had nothing to do with a Guy Fawkes' Night bonfire.

Afterwards, William said that the stench of burning oil was not the only thing he smelt. It may be, though, that he was referring to what his imagination told him must have added a sinister pollutant to the early-morning air.

Rounding the bend, they came upon the remains of a Morris Minor saloon-car parked close to a grassy verge to their right, pointing towards the main road. Flames arched over the roof and lurched fifteen feet above the area of the windscreen.

The heat was so intense that the young men had to sidle along the far verge, their faces averted, before running the 150 yards to Hardingstone, where they parted company for a short time, Alfred going to fetch the village policeman, Bertie Copping, while William roused his father, Hedley, who happened to be the parish constable.

By the time PC Copping arrived at the scene, the flames were less intimidating, and he was able to get close enough to the car to see what looked to him like a black rugby ball on the driver's seat.

William Bailey had had the sense to collect some buckets before dashing back, and a human chain was formed to bring water from a nearby pond. Within a quarter of an hour, the fire was doused – not that, by then, there was much left to burn. The front offside wheel had somehow escaped the flames, but other parts of the vehicle, if not consumed, were contorted and charred.

The roof was completely burnt away, as were the doors and windows, and when the smoke began to clear, PC Copping realized that what he had first thought was a rugby ball was actually a human head. It was face-downwards on the driver's seat. The rest of the blackened body was hard to tell apart from the débris on which it rested, but Copping made out the torso lying across the passenger's seat, with the left arm out of sight beneath the body. The right arm was burnt off at the elbow, and Copping could only surmize that "it had been stretched out horizontally, as though it had been lodged on the back of the seat, which had collapsed during the fire". No more than a stump of the right leg remained. The left leg was doubled up beneath the torso.

Copping shouted to Hedley Bailey to run back to the village and telephone the Northampton police headquarters for assistance.

Things done – or left undone – during the next several hours indicate that the local police force was incredibly, disgracefully inefficient.

Police Inspector James Lawrence and other officers (not a single detective among them) arrived at Hardingstone at about three o'clock, by which time the burnt-out car was no longer smoking. Lawrence had a chat with Copping – from whom he learnt of the mysterious stranger encountered by William Bailey and Alfred Brown – and then proceeded to break so many elementary "don't-touch" investigative rules that one is mystified to understand how he had managed to escape sacking when he was a constable, let alone why he had twice been promoted. (Incidentally, Copping, who accepted Lawrence's crazy decisions without a murmur and who soon afterwards failed to take an obvious action simply because he hadn't been told to, must have bucked his ideas up considerably in later years, for he rose through the ranks to become a superintendent.)

Lawrence subsequently wrote a report, which has never before been quoted from, in which he stated:

> I was suspicious as to the cause of the fire. With assistance, I removed the charred body from the wreckage to the garage of the Crown Inn, Hardingstone, and removed the remains of the car to the grass verge on the side of the road. . . . I observed the registration number as MU 1468. I returned to Northampton and telephoned Scotland Yard to ascertain the name and address of the registered owner of the vehicle.

Before leaving Hardingstone, Lawrence had not given orders for the car to be guarded – and it did not occur to Copping that that would be a sensible precaution. At eight o'clock, when a freelance photographer arrived from Northampton, having been tipped off by someone at police headquarters, the wreckage was being examined by a crowd of villagers. The photographer, Arthur Ashford, arranged some of the remnants to make a more artistic composition, used up a roll of film, and hurried back to his shop to start developing the prints, meanwhile phoning London picture agencies. The response from the agencies was so encouraging that at eleven o'clock Ashford sent his assistant, Edgar Tippleston, to Hardingstone for more snaps. The wreckage was still unguarded.

Though Inspector Lawrence forgot, among other things, to send a police photographer to the scene, he did arrange with a coroner's officer for a doctor to examine the body in the garage. And, as we know, he called Scotland Yard for information regarding the owner of the car.

In the early afternoon, when he returned to Hardingstone to be on hand when the doctor arrived, he had received more details from the Yard than he had expected. He knew that the Morris Minor was the property of a thirty-six-year-old commercial traveller for a firm in Leicester (forty-odd miles north-west of Hardingstone) that made suspenders and garters. The man's name was Alfred Arthur Rouse. According to Rouse's wife, Lily, he had driven away from their house in North London (fifty-odd miles south-east of Hardingstone) at

Hardingstone Lane (looking towards the London Road) on the morning of 6 November, 1930

The burnt-out car

nine o'clock on Guy Fawkes' Night. That – so she said – was the last she had seen of him.

By eight o'clock on the night of Thursday, 6 November, eighteen hours after the discovery of the blazing car, the investigators had concluded that the charred, incomplete corpse that had been stretched across the front seats was that of a murder-victim. The main reason for the conclusion was that – miraculously, considering the extent of the burning – a few scraps of *petrol-soaked* clothing had survived, lodged in the crook formed by the doubled-up left leg and the chest; the doctor who had examined the remains believed that the fire itself, the sheer intensity of the heat, had caused the leg to flex to the body.

And so the Northampton Constabulary issued a press-release, stating that they were anxious to get in touch with the man, dressed like a "city gent", who had been seen near the fire at two o'clock that morning. Whoever composed the release took care not to suggest that Mr Alfred Arthur Rouse, the owner of the car, might be either the "city gent" or the victim.

Rouse, the commercial traveller, had travelled many miles since 2 a.m. After hitching a ride to London from a lorry-driver who had stopped for him on the main road near Hardingstone, he had taken a charabanc to Cardiff, arriving in the Welsh city just in time to catch the last bus to the village of Penybryn, nestling among the mine-pocked hills to the north.

William Jenkins, the proprietor of a small colliery, was expecting Rouse, whom he believed to be his son-in-law. Jenkins's daughter Ivy had returned home to Primrose Villa, Penybryn, at the beginning of October, having spent the past two years as a probationer nurse in London. She had given her family two bits of news: the first – obvious from her appearance – was that she was pregnant; the second was that she had married Arthur Rouse on her twenty-first birthday in June. Arthur had turned up soon afterwards, had at once called Mr Jenkins "Dad", and had led the family to believe that he had paid £125 for a house in Surrey, which, so he said, he was "furnishing beautifully" for his bride. What he had not mentioned, of course, was that he had another house, in

Alfred Arthur Rouse

the district of North London called Friern Barnet, where he and his real wife, Lily, had been living since 1927. He had given Mr Jenkins an address in Victoria, saying that it was his "London *pied-à-terre*"; actually, it was the home of an acquaintance who had agreed to redirect any mail that came for him.

Early in November, Jenkins had needed to write to Rouse at the Victoria address, telling him of complications associated with Ivy's pregnancy. Rouse had replied, first with a telegram asking about Ivy's health, then with a letter saying that he would be coming to see her on the sixth.

As good as his word, Rouse arrived at eight o'clock in the evening. He looked tired. "It has taken me eighteen hours to get here," he told Jenkins. "I've had the car stolen, Dad. It was stolen at Northampton." He went up to see the bedridden Ivy – or "Paddy", as he called her – and Jenkins and his other daughter, Phyllis, prepared a meal. Phyllis had her doubts about Arthur, chiefly because he had tried to make love to her during his first visit.

Rouse tucked into the meal. But his appetite must have been affected by the return of a neighbour who had been in the house when he arrived. The neighbour had come back with a local evening paper. "Is this your car?" he asked Rouse, indicating a briefly-captioned photograph of the burnt-out Morris Minor in Hardingstone Lane. "If it is, you'll see it no more."

Rouse merely glanced at the picture before saying in his high-pitched voice: "That is not my car."

Despite his weariness, he cannot have slept at all soundly that night. At eight o'clock, when he came down for breakfast, he told Jenkins that he had changed his plans: instead of staying over the weekend, he was going back to London at once.

As it happened, a motor-salesman named Hendell Brownhill had driven from Cardiff to arrange a part-exchange deal with Jenkins. He agreed to give Rouse a lift to the city.

Rouse was coming downstairs after saying goodbye to Ivy when a news-boy delivered the *Daily Sketch*. Phyllis took one look at the front page, then showed the paper to Rouse. "Look, Arthur," she said, "here's a photo of your car. It's been burnt."

One almost feels sorry for him. In contrast to the Northampton police, newspapermen throughout the country had immediately sensed that a most unusual crime had been committed in Hardingstone Lane. Photographs taken by the enterprising Arthur Ashford had been reproduced long before the police issued a first, tentative press-release – and that release had prompted further coverage. Though Rouse had travelled hundreds of miles to a remote village in the Welsh hills, there was no escaping the long arm of the press.

Still, he tried to brazen things out. "How do you know it's my car?" he asked Phyllis.

Raising her voice, perhaps because she thought that Arthur was hard of hearing as well as short-sighted, she said, "Your name is there in the report."

He changed the subject. "Take care of Paddy for me," he said. Stuffing the newspaper in his pocket, he got into Brownhill's car and was driven to Cardiff. On the way, Brownhill stopped at the home of another customer. Rouse must have wondered whether there was anyone who had *not* read about "the blazing-car mystery", for the topic came up in after-business conversation. Rouse, usually a chatterbox, remained silent.

Brownhill dropped him at the Great Western coach station. During the day, the car salesman found it hard to think of any car other than the one that had become a funeral-pyre at Hardingstone. At last, at about 8.15 p.m., he spoke to a reporter for a Cardiff newspaper, who, after taking notes of his story, advised him to repeat it to the police.

The information came just in time. Less than a quarter of an hour later, the coach from Cardiff reached Hammersmith Broadway, in West London. A detective, still out of breath after running from the local police station, was waiting on the pavement. He scanned the passengers' faces, then asked "a man with dark hair and a Charlie Chaplin moustache" to alight.

"Are you Mr Rouse?" the detective asked.

"Yes, that's right."

"I should like you to accompany me to the station."

"Very well," Rouse replied. "I'm glad it's all over. I was going to Scotland Yard about it. I'm responsible."

Responsible for a murder? No, that was not what Rouse meant. At the station, after being cautioned, he claimed that on Guy Fawkes' Night he had stopped his car near London to give a lift to a hitch-hiker:

He got in and I drove north. When I had gone some distance, I lost my way. I thought I saw the man's hand on my case, which was in the back of the car. The engine started to spit and I thought I was running out of petrol. I pulled in to the side of the road. I wanted to relieve myself. I said to the man, "There is some petrol in the can. You can empty it into the tank while I am gone." He said, "What about a smoke?" I said, "I have given you all my cigarettes as it is."

I then went some distance along the road and had just got my trousers down when I noticed a big flame from behind. I pulled my trousers up quickly and ran towards the car. I saw the man inside and I tried to open the door but I couldn't as the car was then a mass of flames. I then began to tremble violently, I was all of a shake. I didn't know what to do and I ran as hard as I could along the road, then I saw the two men. I felt I was responsible for what had happened. I lost my head and didn't know what to do and really don't know what I have done since.

After making the statement, Rouse was given a bed in a cell. But he didn't get much rest. In the early hours of the morning, he was driven north, to the Angel Lane police station in Northampton.

There, having been served breakfast, he was taken to the office of Inspector James Lawrence. The fact that Lawrence was completing some paperwork did not stop Rouse from chatting, apparently inconsequentially. He spoke about his wife Lily, saying, "She is really too good for me. I like a woman who will make a fuss of me. I don't ever remember Lily getting on my knee – but otherwise she is a good wife."

A few moments later, still seemingly talking to himself, he said, "I'm very friendly with several women, but it's a very expensive game. My harem takes me to several places, and I'm not at home a great deal."

"*My harem*. . . ." Those words made even the dull-witted James Lawrence sit up. He knew about Ivy Jenkins, but now he wondered whether Rouse had changed the status of other innocent virgins. If so, how many?

It turned out that the answer to that question was astonishing, almost incredible. The answer helped to explain why an unknown man had been cremated in a Morris Minor parked in a country lane.

*   *   *

I shouldn't be surprised if some readers of this story have a special, very personal interest in Alfred Arthur Rouse. I am speaking of women – elderly now, perhaps widowed or married past the Golden mark – who in their youth fell victim to his flattery, false promises and sexual oomph. And there may well be one or two younger readers, women or men, who are quite unaware that they entered the world, or that one of their parents did, as an outcome of Rouse's fecundity.

Towards the end of 1930, when the Northampton police, assisted by other forces, sought to establish the number of girls who had belonged to Rouse's "harem", they hit even more snags than are usual in statistical examinations that depend on "input" from human beings. In sensational criminal cases, the very sensationalism often induces quite innocent people to confess guilt, and prompts others, just as imaginative but less reckless, to claim involvement in events leading up to the main ones. The Rouse case produced a variation on the untrue-confession phenomenon. When word got around (far earlier than was investigatively proper) that Rouse had a "harem", quite a few maidens who were complete strangers to him blushingly revealed how they had succumbed to his animal desires. On the other hand, several girls who really had shared private pleasures with Arthur did not feel inclined to admit their dalliance; some of them may have been dissuaded from chatting about their experiences by picture-paper reports on "Rouse and his Harem" which made membership of the latter body sound only slightly less exclusive than membership of the Ovaltineys, the Keep Fit League, or the Independent Order of Oddfellows.

A senior detective on the case reckoned that, give or take a dozen or so, Rouse had "achieved illicit conquest" of 80 women during the 1920s. Rouse himself was not much help with the arithmetic. He had not kept a tally of his lady-friends – nor of how many of them (or, of each of those, how often) had been so harem-scarem that they had been put to the inconvenience of curtailing expectancy or had actually become maternal. When he was asked if he could quantify his illegitimate offspring, he did a quick sum in his head, then hazarded: "Eight or ten – *to my knowledge*."

It has been suggested that, at the time of his marriage in

H. M. PRISON, *Bedford*

nov 11 19 *25*

Reg. *796 A. A. Rouse.*

With reference to the statements as to above-named prisoner's health in the accompanying letter, I have to report that

his health is good

[signature]
Medical Officer.

Forwarded   *[signature]*

Governor.

No. 596

(10852—98-13-09)

In replying to this letter, please write on the envelope:—

Number 796 Name A Rouse

Bedford Prison

11 . 11 . 1930

My Dear Wife,

If you could possibly
manage to do so, could you see me here
as soon as you can as there are many
things to be done. I am allowed
fifteen minutes private conversation
with you. I cannot write a great
deal as you must know how upset I
am to have brought all this
trouble on you, the best woman
God ever gave man.

I received your letter
also one from my Dad, for which
I am grateful.

Kiss Arthur for me and
try to think kindly of me.

Have you got the cheque
from Abermanbury. I am writing

No 24

(8252—20-4-00)

18

after this to Leicester, to ask
them to send to you any
moneys due or about to become
due. I should advertise the home
for sale as you will want all
the money you can get. The
insurance on car you cannot touch
at all.

However if you can
come and see me I will
explain all. I cannot eat the
food not that it matters much, but
before seeing me if you enquire what
you can give me you would
certainly help my lot here.

Butter is my worst miss.
However, you had better enquire here
first, before seeing me.

Your husband
Arthur

November 1914 – he was then twenty, his wife twenty-three – he had a "normal appetite for sex", and that his subsequent gluttony was somehow whetted by his having been wounded in the temple while soldiering in France (because of the injury, he was discharged from the army in the following year, 1916). But the notion is dented by the fact that he put a French girl in the family way within days of his arrival in France, less than four months after his marriage to Lily Watkins.

It seems to me that a more probable cause-and-effect explanation for his ex-service philandering is that his new occupation of commercial travelling entailed a majority of bed-times away from his proper bed, and provided a temptation, which he was pleased to deem irresistible, to have a number of girls in every port of call.

Though he had not seen his mother since she had walked out on his Irish-born father in 1900, he told girls he met on his travels that he had "just spent a weekend with mater at our place in the country"; though he had been educated at

---

Text of letter:

My Dear Wife,

If you could possibly manage to do so, could you see me here as soon as you can as there are many things to be done. I am allowed fifteen minutes private conversation with you. I cannot write a great deal as you must know how upset I am to have brought all this trouble on you, the best woman God ever gave man.

I received your letter also one from my Dad, for which I am grateful.

Kiss Arthur for me and try to think kindly of me.

Have you got the cheque from Aldermanbury. I am writing after this to Leicester, to ask them to send you any moneys due or about to become due. I should advertize the house for sale as you will want all the money you can get. The insurance on car you cannot touch at all.

However if you can come and see me I will explain all. I cannot eat the food not that it matters much, but before seeing me if you can enquire what you can give me you would certainly help my lot here.

Butter is my worse miss. However, you had better enquire here first, before seeing me.

Your husband
ARTHUR

Another of Rouse's letters was shown to a graphologist, who (so it was said) was given no hint as to who had written it. The graphologist declared: "The writer is insincere, secretive, has a bad conscience; is evasive, plausible, a braggart, vain, clever, glib, shrewd; is a business man without principle, a clever talker, yet suffers from an inferiority complex."

state schools, he claimed to be a product of Eton and
Cambridge; though he had never risen from the rank of private
in the Queen's Territorial Regiment, he said that he had been
invalided out of the army as a major; though, apart from a
tiny service-pension, his sole income was from the touting of
gadgets of an uplifting nature (a spokesman for his employers
would testify that "his salary was £4 a week, £1 fixed expenses,
plus actual expenses, plus commission"), he gave the
impression, or tried to, that he had substantial private means.

One of his first post-war conquests was also probably the
youngest – a fourteen-year-old Scottish girl, Helen Campbell,
who by the time she was fifteen had borne him a child in a
London home for unmarried mothers. The child died when
only five weeks old, and Helen returned to her job as a
domestic servant of one of Rouse's few male friends. A couple
of years later, Rouse again made Helen pregnant. This time,
belatedly refusing to take things lying down, she told him that
he had to marry her. After a church-wedding – considered
binding by Helen, who had been led to believe that Rouse
was now divorced – the couple moved into a flat in Liverpool
Road, Islington (about five miles south-east of his real matri-
monial home in Buxted Road, Friern Barnet). Rouse used his
job as the excuse for being away much of the time; in fact, of
course, he was travelling some days, living with Lily on others.
Following the birth of the child, a boy, Rouse and Helen had
a difference of opinion, and they parted, she keeping the child.
She brought maintenance proceedings against Rouse, and he
was ordered to pay her ten shillings a week.

Subsequently, Rouse owned up to Lily: not about all of his
extra-marital sexcapades – just about his association with
Helen Campbell. Far from indicating a guilty conscience, the
confession was entirely practical, aimed at staving off prosecution for being in arrears with the maintenance payments.
His spiel won Lily over – to the extent that she agreed to look
after the illegitimate child as if it were her own. Presumably,
Rouse had already agreed the arrangement with Helen, having
mentioned, in passing, that he had married her bigamously;
in any event, the little boy was handed over and was still being
fostered by Lily when his father became a celebrity.

As an important aside, it must be said that there are reasons
for suspecting that Lily Rouse knew of her husband's plan to

commit murder. If his hope was that the burnt body would be identified as his own, thus allowing him to start a new life, freed from the tangle of troubles he had created for himself, he may well have sought Lily's aid. Shortly before the murder, the Rouses had discussed separation; and at about the same time, Rouse had arranged additional "life cover" in his car insurance. Lily may have preferred the hope of receiving a very large lump-sum from the insurance company to the prospect of continually having to force Arthur to keep up payments on a separation allowance. When a London detective visited her following the discovery of the funeral-pyre near Northampton, she did not mention that she had seen her husband shortly before, when he had called at the house to change his clothes prior to travelling to Wales to see his expectant "wife", Ivy Jenkins; and after she had been taken to Northampton much later in the day – but before it was established that Rouse was very much alive – she said that brace-buckles and other small metal objects found among the burnt human remains "might" be her husband's.

But to return to earlier events: in 1928, quite by chance, Lily had discovered that Arthur was carrying on with another girl. In the spring of that year, she asked him to take her to a nearby theatre to see a murder-play. Sorry, he said; he could not afford such luxuries – anyway, he had a business appointment that night. Lily decided that if she scrimped and saved on the housekeeping expenses (Rouse allowed her £2 a week), she could just about afford a seat in the gallery for the second performance. While she was standing in the queue, she saw Arthur coming out after the first house, arm-in-arm with a young woman who was noticeably pregnant. Lily created quite a scene, ignoring Arthur's offer to make polite introductions, and so he hurried his companion to his car and drove away.

The expectant girl's name was Nellie Tucker. Like Helen Campbell, she was a domestic servant. And, again like Helen, she was one of Rouse's long-running sources of pleasure. He had first met her in 1925, when she was seventeen. She gave birth to his child, a daughter, soon after the first, unintended meeting with Lily. A year or so later, Rouse having virtually ignored the maintenance order against him, she handed the baby over to a foster-mother – and promptly became pregnant again.

She gave birth to a second girl-child by Rouse in a maternity hospital in City Road, London, on 29 October 1930. Adding to Rouse's difficulties, the hospital authorities insisted on having some sort of proof that Nellie was married. So, posing as his own brother, he went to the church where he had bigamously married Helen Campbell and obtained a copy of the marriage certificate; the reason he gave for wanting the document was that Mr Alfred Arthur Rouse had just been burned to death in a car accident.

He visited Nellie at the hospital on Guy Fawkes' Night, arriving at seven o'clock and staying about an hour. Nellie noticed that he was not his usual cheery self. She asked him what was wrong, and he said that he had so many debts that he hardly knew where to turn. That was only a part-explanation; among his other worries was the fact that Ivy Jenkins, the member of his "harem" who was next in line to bear him a child, was seriously ill at her home in Wales. And, almost certainly, he was being threatened with blackmail by someone who had learned of his bigamy.

He kept looking at his watch, and when Nellie asked if he had an appointment, said that he had to drive north on business.

The business he had in mind, that Guy Fawkes' Night, involved using his car for a bonfire in which a man of his own height and build would be the guy.

Some twenty-five years ago, when Lord Birkett was interviewed by John Freeman in the first of the "Face to Face" television programmes, he said that two murder trials stood out in his memory: in one, that of Dr Buck Ruxton at Manchester in 1936, he led for the defence; in the other, that of Alfred Arthur Rouse at Northampton in January 1931, he was the prosecutor.

There was so much evidence to show that Rouse had committed the "blazing-car murder" that Norman Birkett decided not to call Helen Campbell and to restrict his examination of Nellie Tucker to questions concerning the time at which Rouse left her on the eve of the murder. Although Birkett believed that the girls' stories were relevant, in that they aided the Crown's contention that Rouse had intended the charred body in the car to be mistaken for his own, thus allowing him to escape the consequences of his immorality, there was a risk that such testimony would be considered irrelevantly prejudicial by the Court of Criminal Appeal. No doubt Birkett's decision was influenced by the fact that the girls' stories were already common knowledge, for their evidence at the committal proceedings had been reported verbatim in the national (indeed, *inter*national) press.

Birkett's overall task was simple enough – but it would have been simpler still if the Northampton police had acted at all efficiently following the discovery of the burning car in Hardingstone Lane.

As no notes or measurements had been taken before the body was carted away, there was uncertainty about its position across the front seats of the Morris Minor – and even about the extent of the burning. Of the three policemen who had perfunctorily examined the body before it was moved, one recalled that the right leg was burnt off at the knee, another that the leg was severed about halfway between the ankle and the knee, and the third that only the foot had been consumed.

As the car was left unguarded for at least eight hours, the notes made subsequently regarding the presence and position of detached parts and contents of the vehicle could not be relied upon.

Lacking a single police-photograph of the wreckage, Birkett was obliged to produce as exhibits photographs taken by Arthur Ashford, the Northampton man who worked as a freelance for press picture-agencies. It was most upsetting for Birkett that he had to call Ashford as his first witness, to "prove" the photographs. This allowed Douglas Finnemore, Rouse's counsel, to score some early points – though perhaps more at the expense of the police than on behalf of his client. After getting Ashford to say that several people were looking at the wrecked car when he arrived in Hardingstone Lane, Finnemore pointed out that whereas the steering-wheel was lying on the ground in some of the photographs, it was on the steering-column in others . . . that one photograph showed the branch of a tree hanging across the back of the car while another showed nothing of the sort . . . and so on. Ashford – who, incidentally, had made a small fortune from the sale of

Norman Birkett, KC

the pictures – was more concerned with protecting his reputation as an accurate photographer than with being a truthful
witness; but in the end he had to agree that he had rearranged
one or two things in the cause of artistry. His insistence that

he was not responsible for all of the differences earned bе points for the defence, since, as Mr Finnemore took pains to emphasize to the jury, the implication was that other unofficial hands had done a spot of rearranging.

When Mr Finnemore sat down, Rouse leaned across the rail of the dock and murmured an optimistic remark to his solicitor. Then, smiling broadly, he looked around the court and nodded to a number of women spectators, some of whom he knew extremely well. He was dressed in a new pin-striped suit, bought for him by his wife Lily, who sat close to the dock.

After the cross-examination of Arthur Ashford, Rouse had no reason for cheerfulness. One after another, the prosecution witnesses entered the court, said what Birkett wanted them to say, answered defence questions politely but unhelpfully, then departed. Thirty-four of them in all, including the two young men who had seen Rouse in Hardingstone Lane while the fire was raging, the lorry-driver who had given him a lift to London, people who had met him during his curtailed visit to South Wales and observed his reactions – or rather, non-reactions – to newspaper pictures of his wrecked car. (None of the Welsh witnesses was allowed to mention that Rouse had travelled to the village of Penybryn to see his pregnant "wife", Ivy Jenkins.)

The star prosecution witness was Colonel Cuthbert Buckle, a fire-assessor who had examined the remaining mechanical parts of the Morris Minor and noted, among much else, that a nut on the union-joint of the petrol-pipe was one whole turn loose. The colonel was convinced that the nut had been intentionally loosened so as to increase the flow of petrol feeding the fire in the area near the passenger-seat. He talked like a textbook, impressing everyone in court, especially those who were baffled by his science.

As soon as Buckle's evidence was reported in the press, Rouse's solicitor received two phone calls, the first from a London motor-engineer named Arthur Isaacs, the second from Arthur Cotton, a resident of Chorlton-cum-Hardy, Manchester, who acted as a fire-assessor for fifteen insurance companies. Both men said that, in their experience, the nut on the union joint was *always* loosened by intense heat. Cotton added that, only the day before, he had examined a burnt-out

…chester and found the union-nut loosened
… solicitor arranged for the men to come to
… appear as witnesses for the defence.

…st to go into the witness box, answered Douglas
Fr… questions convincingly. Then Norman Birkett
stood… He was determined to discredit Isaacs. It didn't
matter to him if he misled the jury in doing so.

"What is the coefficient of the expansion of brass?" he
asked.

Isaacs looked bemused. "The what?"

"The coefficient of the expansion of brass," Birkett
repeated.

"I'm afraid I cannot answer."

"Do you know what the question means?"

"Well, if you put it that way, I don't."

Ignoring that reply – and ignoring the fact that a Crown
counsel's primary duty is to get at the truth rather than to get
a conviction – Birkett continued to ask about the coefficient
of the expansion of brass, giving the impression that Isaacs'
bewilderment showed him up as a charlatan. As Isaacs'
discomfort increased, so did the laughter from the public
gallery.

Arthur Cotton was tortured in much the same way. It is said
that, because of the publicity given to his apparent ignorance,
a number of his clients cancelled their contracts with him.

But in discrediting Isaacs and Cotton, Birkett had brought
discredit on himself. The answer to the question (0.0000189)
was known to very few fire-loss assessors; it had virtually
no practical relevance. Birkett had framed the question after
scanning heat-factor tables in a book provided by Colonel
Buckle. Many years later, still refusing to admit that he had
been at all unfair, he said that if, by a thousand-to-one chance,
either Isaacs or Cotton had known the answer, he would have
changed the subject from brass to copper, then to aluminium,
eventually pretending that the answer was of no importance[1].

Rouse gave evidence on his own behalf. At the start, when

---

1. When this article first appeared, serialized in the *Manchester Evening News*, I
commented at this point that, so far as I was aware, the controversy over whether
Buckle was right to infer that the union-nut had been deliberately loosened had
never been resolved, and I said that I should like to hear from fire-assessors who
had views on the matter. A letter I received is reproduced, in part, on page 33.

he was being coaxed along by his counsel, he clearly enjoyed the opportunity of talking about himself. But his answer to one of Mr Finnemore's first questions illustrates that lucidity was not among his strong points. Referring to his army service, he said, "I joined up on 8 August, I think it was, and I was wounded on 15 April. I believe it was February. 25 May 1915, I think it was."

Other answers were just as opaque. And there were times when, instead of giving the simple "yes" or "no" answer that his counsel wanted, he rambled irrelevantly.

Often his conceit caused him to display knowledge that he would have been better off keeping to himself – no more so than when, during the long cross-examination by Norman Birkett, he revealed that he was a mine of information on risks associated with petroleum. As somebody commented afterwards: "One felt that if *he* had been asked about the coefficient of the expansion of brass, he would have given the correct answer."

Towards the end of the cross-examination, there were times when Rouse was almost incoherent. But, despite the merciless probing, he continued to insist that he was relieving himself behind a hedge when his car, and the unknown passenger, had gone up in flames.

As he walked back to the dock, he stole a glance at the jury, perhaps hoping for a sign that one or other of the dozen men had been impressed by his performance. But the jurymen simply stared back, giving no indication of the verdict they had in mind.

The trial ended on Saturday, 31 January 1931, a day of wind, sleet and snow. Despite the inclement weather, people started queuing for the public gallery in the lovely Northampton Assize Court before dawn; comparatively few were admitted, and the rest, many of them women, settled down to a long, uncomfortable wait for the verdict. By mid-morning, the crowd had grown so large that mounted policemen were needed to keep the road clear.

Perhaps it was the blustery wind that caused the flag above the court-building to make a gradual descent so that it was at half-mast by the time the jury retired to consider the verdict. That was at a quarter past two. Before starting their life-or-death discussion, the twelve men took light refreshments and then spent a few minutes looking at the burnt-out Morris Minor in an enclosed courtyard. They didn't talk for long. At half-past three, a trumpet heralded their return.

The court quickly filled. The only place that remained empty was the seat near the dock that Lily Rouse had occupied during the previous five days. At the end of the proceedings on the Friday, Rouse had snapped his fingers at Lily and pointed to his neck – not, as most of the spectators assumed, to signify his resignation to a gallows-death, but to indicate that he needed a clean collar. And so Lily had traipsed the town to find an outfitter's shop that was still open, and early on the final day had walked to the court-building to leave a packet of half a dozen new collars for her husband. Her extravagance in buying more collars than the one he had requested was her way of implying confidence that he would be acquitted – an implication weakened by a note she enclosed in the packet, saying that her nerves were so frayed that she could not face being in court that day.

Compensating for Lily's absence, some members of Rouse's harem were present when the Clerk of Assize asked the foreman of the jury: "Do you find the prisoner guilty or not guilty of murder?".

The minute the answer was given, a reporter for a national news-agency slipped out of the court and ran towards a window facing the Black Boy Hotel; he was carrying two handkerchiefs, one red for "Guilty", the other white for "Not Guilty". In an upstairs room of the hotel, a colleague was waiting for the signal, ready to shout one word or two over an open telephone-line to London. The reporter waved the red handkerchief.

Rouse's only visible reaction to the verdict was a slight shrug of the shoulders. In marked contrast, Helen Campbell and Nellie Tucker wept uncontrollably and had to be assisted from the court; there were shrieks and moans from women in the gallery.

When the Clerk of Assize asked Rouse if he had anything to say why judgment of death should not be pronounced, Rouse hesitated a moment, then replied: "Only that I am innocent, sir."

Considering that the judge, Mr Justice Talbot, had referred

to Rouse as "a most facile liar" during his summing-up, it is unlikely that he took much notice of the protestation of innocence; even so, he appeared to be on the verge of tears as he passed the mandatory sentence.

Rouse did not seem at all upset. He was smiling as he turned to leave the dock, and he waved to reporters in the grand-jury box and to the red-eyed women in the gallery before descending the steps to the cells. Soon afterwards, he was taken in a Black Maria to Bedford Gaol, where the Governor, anticipating the verdict, had arranged for the condemned cell, used only three times in the past sixty years, to be given a fresh coat of whitewash.

In the evening, Rouse sat on his cot, staring gloomily into space. One of the warders on the "death watch" suggested a game of cards, but he shook his head and muttered something about "three Sundays" – presumably a reference to the custom of allowing three Sundays to pass before a death sentence was carried out.

But Rouse's life was to be prolonged. Shortly after the trial, his solicitor announced that there was to be an appeal – conducted by Sir Patrick Hastings, who was probably the most highly-paid barrister in the country. Expense was no object. The Rouse case had made "chequebook journalism" big business: popular national papers had paid large amounts in advance for the "innermost secrets" of some of the fallen women – and had paid far more for just a few words from Lily.

The main ground of the appeal, heard at the Royal Courts of Justice in London on 23 February, was unusual in that it referred to matters that had not been mentioned at the trial. Sir Patrick Hastings argued that Rouse had been gravely prejudiced by the fact that statements he had volunteered to the police regarding his sex-life had been read out during the committal proceedings "and published throughout the length and breadth of Britain, making him seem a man of terrible, abnormal immorality".

Hastings also argued that the jury had been misled by the evidence of Colonel Cuthbert Buckle, the fire assessor who had testified that the union-nut on the Morris Minor's petrol-feed pipe had been deliberately loosened, thus feeding the flames. Hastings claimed that, since the trial, the defence had heard from "literally hundreds of engineers and scientists" who supported the loosening-by-heat theory, and he asked leave to call two of them. After conferring, the appeal judges turned down the request "because both points of view were clearly before the jury".

Other arguments put forward by Hastings were insubstantial, and, though two of the three judges expressed concern about some aspects of the pre-trial publicity, the appeal was dismissed.

Now Rouse could only hope that the Home Secretary, John Clynes, would grant a reprieve. The defence lawyers delivered a request for a re-examination of the facts of the case to the Home Office, and this was followed by a petition with thousands of signatures. In a telephone call to the Home Secretary's wife, Lily insisted: "I know Arthur is innocent."

All in vain. Mr Clynes said that he could see no reason for intervening.

On Monday, 9 March, the day before the execution, the *Daily Express* published a statement from Lily: "I have been seeing Arthur constantly, and he has consistently protested his innocence." That night, she travelled to Bedford Gaol for the last time. While she was talking to her husband, Helen Campbell turned up. Lily left her husband alone with his mistress for twenty minutes, then went back to say, "Goodbye, Daddy, I'm sorry it has to be like this."

Just before eight o'clock next morning, Rouse was carried, screaming and struggling, to the gallows. However, as soon as the mask was pulled over his face, he became calm, or at least still, and the execution was carried out exactly at the appointed time.

The following day, his confession appeared in the *Daily Sketch*. Although his account of how he had set fire to the car was questioned, and still is, there is little doubt that the rest of the confession was true; a couple of rival dailies insisted that the whole thing was a fabrication, but that was only natural, since they had been outbid for it by the *Sketch*. One of the pooh-poohing papers, the *Express*, was given another reason for pique when, on the Sunday following the appearance of the confession, the *News of the World* published a letter written by Lily on 7 March – two days before the *Express* had printed her statement that Rouse had "consistently protested his innocence" – in which she said that Rouse had told her before the appeal that he was guilty.

In his confession, Rouse said that he had intended the police to think that it was he who had perished in the fire: "I was in a tangle in various ways. . . . I was fed up. I wanted to start afresh." In October 1930, he had come across his victim, "a down-and-out", at the Swan & Pyramids pub[2] in Whetstone High Road, close to his home; he had treated the man to beer, he himself drinking lemonade (as he was a teetotaller as well as a non-smoker). He had decided that the man "was the sort no one would miss . . . I thought he would suit the plan I had in mind. . . . I suddenly realized that I should do it on 5 November, which was Bonfire Night, when a fire would not be noticed so much." On 2 or 3 November, he had again met the man at the Swan & Pyramids: "When I said that I intended to go to Leicester on the Wednesday night [the 5th], he said he would be glad of a lift up there. This was what I thought he would say. I made an appointment with him for the Wednesday night for about eight o'clock. I met him outside the Swan & Pyramids, and we went into the bar. . . . I bought a bottle of whisky. Then we both got into the car, which was outside the public-house.

"We drove first of all to my house in Buxted Road. I got out, leaving the man in the car. My wife was in. She had seen me draw up near the house and she asked me who it was I had in the car. I said it was a man I knew, but she suspected that it was a woman. I said, "All right. I'll drive up in front of the house, as I am turning around, to let you see that it is a man." I did so, as I drove out of Buxted Road, so that my wife could see for herself and would have no grounds for jealousy. So far as I remember, it was about 8.30 when I started off for the north with the man in the car. . . . During the journey, the man drank the whisky neat from the bottle and was getting quite fuzzled.

"I turned into Hardingstone Lane because it was quiet and near a main road, where I could get a lift from a lorry afterwards. . . . The man was half-dozing – the effect of the whisky. I looked at him and then gripped him by the throat

2. Bulwer Lytton probably had this place in mind when he wrote the tavern scenes of *Paul Clifford*, his novel (published in 1830) about a sometimes-chivalrous highwayman.

with my right hand. I pressed his head against the back of the seat. He slid down, his hat falling off. I saw he had a bald patch on the crown of his head. He just gurgled. I pressed his throat hard. . . . He did not resist. It was all very sudden. The man did not realize what was happening. I pushed his face back. After making a peculiar noise, the man was silent."

Rouse said that he then doused the car and the body with petrol from a full can he had brought with him. He asserted that, before starting the fire, he "loosened the petrol union-nut and took the top off the carburettor". (Of course, the reference to the union-nut did not end the controversy regarding Colonel Buckle's "deliberate act" testimony at the trial: those who disagreed with the colonel's inference argued that, if Rouse really did loosen the nut, he simply anticipated the effect of the heat.)

Rouse ended the confession by saying that he had no idea of the identity of his victim. "I never asked him his name. There was no reason why I should do so."

A week after the publication of the confession, the charred and shrivelled remains of the unidentified man were buried in the churchyard at Hardingstone. The vicar conducted a simple service, and later he and his wife planted crocuses from their garden on the grave.

An appeal for contributions towards the cost of a headstone was poorly supported, raising only enough to buy a rough oak cross bearing the inscription,

IN MEMORY OF AN UNKNOWN MAN
DIED NOV 6th 1930.

Postscript

A. J. Cotton, Son & Partners. . . .
> *557 Barlow Moor Road*
> *Chorlton-cum-Hardy*
> *Manchester M21 2AL*

8 August 1983

Mr Jonathan Goodman,
c/o The Manchester Evening News,
Deansgate, Manchester

Dear Sir,

I have read with avid interest your series on the case of Alfred Arthur Rouse and in particular the part in which you dealt with the technical aspects of this trial and asked to hear from present-day practitioners with views on the matter.

As you will see from this letter-heading, the firm started by Arthur John Cotton in 1921 is still "alive and kicking"; my partner Mr Dennis Ashmore and I, after having been in partnership with Mr E. Kevin Cotton, who was Arthur Cotton's son, purchased the practice from his family upon his unfortunately early death in 1973. . . . I would like to reply to the points raised in your article, which I found to be a very fair representation of the case as I know it, on behalf of the company. I note that you would like to hear the views of present-day "fire-assessors" on this matter, and before I start I would like to mention certain facts.

I have been very well aware of the case of Regina *v.* Alfred Arthur Rouse for many years. In fact, it is a classic example of the role of an expert witness in court. I spend a large part of my time, and have done so for the last 20 or more years, in all the courts of this country, giving expert evidence on all matters relating to automobile engineering and accidents, both on the road involving motor vehicles and in factories. I think that I can justifiably claim to be a reasonably competent expert witness, as will no doubt be confirmed by any practitioners, some of whom are High Court Judges, Queen's Counsel, junior Counsel and Solicitors, in the courts of this country and in particular the Manchester area. I am at present National President Elect of the Institute of Automotive Engineer

Assessors. . . . Unfortunately, I only met Arthur Cotton on one occasion, just prior to his death in 1959, and cannot speak as to his views on the case of Rouse.

I have, however, over the years read of this and other cases of similar nature in considerable detail and I must say that your account is certainly one of the most accurate I have read. Both I and numerous members of my profession are aware of the fate which Arthur Cotton met at the hands of Mr Norman Birkett, KC, during the trial. In fact, it is held up as an example of the manner in which expert evidence should not be given. In reply to Mr Birkett's question regarding the coefficient of expansion of brass, Mr Cotton should have replied along the following lines:

"This is information I do not keep in my head; I will have to consult the engineering authorities on the matter, and require notice of such a question." Any King's (or Queen's) Counsel would immediately recognize the fairness of such a reply, as nobody would ask him similar technical questions on matters of Law and expect him to answer them "off the top of his head".

However, Mr Birkett, as became his great reputation, more so as a defender than a prosecutor, was in my opinion perfectly entitled to ask such a question of an expert witness.

Colonel Buckle having been called as the prosecution expert, the defence were certainly entitled to call similar expert evidence, more so because in those days their client's life was at stake. Matters then were apparently not as they are today, because if a man now faces a major charge such as murder, the defence will leave no stone unturned in order to establish a defence; today, any Member of our Institute faced with a similar problem would undoubtedly insist on technical tests being undertaken in order to establish the point.

From my personal reading of the case over the years, and in particular your excellent article, I am convinced that Mr Rouse was guilty of the murder of the tramp and was justifiably convicted and executed. However, it would appear that the defence was by no means properly organized insofar as the expert evidence appears to have been called very hurriedly without proper consultation with the defence lawyers having taken place.

To turn to the more technical aspects of the matter: it would appear that here we are dealing with a Morris Minor car which apparently had a gravity-fed petrol system with the petrol tank being mounted above the driver's feet, on the scuttle panel, with a copper pipe running firstly inside the car from the bottom of the tank, through the bulkhead and to the carburettor. The pipe would undoubtedly have been made of copper and secured to the underside of the petrol tank by means of a male brass union, an olive, also made of brass, and a brass nut.

I have had very considerable experience in investigating motor-vehicle fires and indeed am the author of the standard authority on the subject of "Automobile Assessing", which is the title of my book published by Butterworths in 1983. I cannot concur with the opinion of Mr Isaacs or Mr Cotton in this matter. In my view, a brass union-nut and a brass union on to which it is screwed will both expand at the same rate and will not become loose. The copper pipe may well melt under intense heat, but – and this is subject to practical tests – the two parts of the brass union-nut will not separate, let alone be loosened to the extent of one whole turn. Again, I return to the point that practical tests should have been undertaken in this case, particularly as the defendant's life was at stake, although I readily acknowledge that the evidence against Rouse from other sources was probably the basis of the jury's conviction.

I feel sure that had the trial judge received an application for an adjournment so that practical tests could be undertaken, bearing in mind that both Mr Isaacs and Mr Cotton only learned of the case a short time before they gave evidence, it would have been granted. It does not appear to me that the defence was generally conducted in a manner in which it would be today. The prosecution saw fit to call Colonel Buckle, who in fact examined the car, and I find it inconceivable that the defence were not aware of the fact that Colonel Buckle was to give evidence, and therefore in their client's interests they should have arranged for the best expert evidence to be available, long before the hearing. As I understand it, Colonel Buckle's evidence must have been available at the committal proceedings.

Having said all that, I readily acknowledge that the availability of experts in those days was not what it is today. The art has grown into a fully-fledged profession and there are a number of eminent experts in the Manchester area alone who are capable of giving evidence of a very high order in cases such as this.

I hope that the foregoing remarks will be of interest to you. To summarise: on the evidence which is now available, I do not feel that it could be established beyond reasonable doubt that Rouse loosened the petrol union, although his motives for doing so were quite obvious; this was the obvious source of the admission of petrol into the car prior to its being ignited, and, fortunately for the poor unknown victim, he is not likely to have known anything about his demise. . . .

Yours faithfully,
p.p. A. J. Cotton, Son & Partners.[3]

DAVID GRIFFITHS, T. Eng (CEI), MInstAEA,
  MIMI, MInstBE, FCIArb.

---

3. Since this letter was written, the partnership has been dissolved, and David Griffiths has begun practising on his own account, from the same address, as Cotton Griffiths & Co.

Fire-lit Tales of Murder

Richard Whittington-Egan

IT WAS THE bitterest January night that, even up there on the savage-toothed northern heights of Northumberland, they had known for years.

Tuesday, 6 January 1931. Twelfth Night. The dead end of Christmas. A clear, star-flecked sky – like a cold sarcophagus lid.

The little country bus returning shortly before ten o'clock from Newcastle to home-base, Foster's Garage, Otterburn, chugged and steamed across rough, tussocky moorland, frozen stiff as corrugated-iron and magpied with great splotches of frost that glittered grittily in the cold blaze of moonlight.

There were no passengers. Only the driver, Cecil Johnstone, and his conductor, Thomas Rutherford.

They had just passed through the small sliced crag of moorland backbone known as Wolf's Nick when they saw the eerie orange glow. It was on the moor – away to the right.

Johnstone decided to investigate. Rutherford stayed behind in the bus.

A short, slithering distance across the ice-polished heather, he came to the source of the fire. A burnt-out car.

Approaching closer, Johnstone stood suddenly rooted by the shock of recognition. The car, a Hudson Super-Six, TN 8135, belonged to his boss's daughter, Evelyn Foster.

Heart thumping, dreading what he might see, he peered into the smouldering interior. To his intense relief it was empty.

His relief was short-lived. From somewhere out of the near-darkness came a kind of thin, rustling moan.

Johnstone, joined now by Rutherford, shuffled unwillingly forward, nine or ten leaden-footed yards, to where a dark shape lay twisting and twitching on the ground.

It was Evelyn Foster . . . transformed into a human torch . . . burning against the ice.

Horrified, they saw that the twenty-nine-year-old girl had been virtually split in two by the ferocious alchemy of the flames. Half of her – the lower half – seemed little more than charcoal. The upper part of her body, dreadfully burned and disfigured as it was, had somehow retained its intactness, and, although obviously muddled and dazed by the terrible pain that she had suffered, her brain was working with extraordinary clearness. Dehydrated, burnt dry, tortured by thirst, she was sucking desperately at the ice on the ground.

Naturally, Johnstone and Rutherford thought that she had had an accident. But that, according to Evelyn Foster, was not the way of it at all. As Johnstone knelt down beside her and wrapped her poor charred body in his overcoat, she whispered, "It was that awful man. Oh, that awful man."

Johnstone gathered her up gently in his arms and carried her to the bus.

"It's all right now," he said. "We're taking you home."

Home was the village of Otterburn, where the Foster family owned a thriving bus and car-hire business, and lived in a comfortable house – "The Kennels" – just across the road from Foster's Garage.

They put Evelyn to bed, and a doctor and a district nurse were summoned. Also the police.

After examining his patient, the doctor told her mother that there was nothing he could do for her. And, indeed, Evelyn Foster had only a handful of hours of life left. But during those hours she gasped in intervals of anguished consciousness a story which must rate as one of the most perplexing criminological riddles of the century.

She was, she said, at about seven o'clock on that Tuesday evening, driving back to Otterburn in her hire-car, having just taken three passengers to the village of Rochester. It was as she was passing through Elishaw, a couple of miles north of Otterburn, that she had been hailed by some people in a stationary car at the roadside.

There were two – or perhaps three, she was not clear – men and a woman in the car. One of the men got out and came across to her. He told her that earlier that day he had missed the Edinburgh-to-Newcastle bus at Jedburgh, but that the people in the car had given him a lift as far as Elishaw. Now, however, they were turning off to Hexham, but they said he would be able to pick up a bus in Otterburn which would take him the final stage of his journey to Newcastle.

Evelyn told him that in fact the last bus from Otterburn to Newcastle had already gone, but she would give him a lift into Otterburn, and might be able to run him on to Ponteland, where he could get a bus to Newcastle. The charge for the twenty-four-mile trip to Ponteland would be about £2.

When she and the man reached Otterburn, Evelyn had dropped him at the village inn, the Percy Arms, while she went to the garage to fill up.

She then drove back to the Percy Arms.

The man was waiting for her beside the bridge there. He climbed into the front seat next to her, lit a cigarette, and off they went, heading for Ponteland.

As they sped smoothly across the moors they chatted amiably. The man, speaking with a north-country accent and smoking incessantly, said that he lived in the Midlands and did not know much about Newcastle. He did seem to know quite a lot about cars, though, and said he had one of his own.

They had just reached Belsay, six miles from Ponteland, when, suddenly, the man ordered, "Turn here and go back."

"Why go back when you've come so far?" asked Evelyn.

"That's got nothing to do with you," was the curt reply.

The man's whole manner had undergone a frightening change.

Now he was creeping along the seat towards her . . . and seized the steering-wheel.

"Oh, no," she said, pushing him off. "I'll do the driving."

He didn't answer. Just fetched her a stinging blow to the eye and shoved her roughly over to the side of the car, pinioning her there as he drove back in silence in the direction of Otterburn.

At Wolf's Nick he stopped. And, with a kind of lunatic inappropriateness, said, "Have a cigarette."

When she refused it, he smirked, "You *are* an independent young woman."

Then he started attacking her again. He hit her, kicked her, and finally knocked her into the back of the car, where, as she told her mother, he interfered with her.

After that, she lost consciousness.

The next thing she remembered was a vague awareness that he had taken something – perhaps a bottle or tin – from his pocket and was pouring its contents over her.

Then . . . a great swoosh of flame . . . and she was burning. . . .

The car now seemed to be jolting over rough ground. The bumping roused her. She was in a furnace. Suffocating. She managed to open the car door and roll herself out on to the moorland.

Lying there under the stars, she thought she heard a car draw up. She thought she heard a whistle. But she could not be sure. Then . . . nothing. The stars fell to become dancing ice pebbles on the great black moorland sheet of . . . nothing. . . .

Evelyn Foster slipped quietly away into that star-speckled nothingness at half-past seven the following morning.

Her last words were: "I have been murdered. Mother, I have been murdered."

The dead girl had described her killer. Age about 25 or 30. Clean-shaven. Slim. Dapper. Plausible. Height a little over five feet six inches. Very respectable and gentlemanly-like – "a bit of a knut". Wearing a bowler-hat and dark suit and dark overcoat.

The hunt for him was on.

With every confidence, the Northumberland police set about combing the frostbound wilderness for the man in the bowler-hat.

But, as clue after clue melted away like the ice-water, the bright edge of confidence became more and more tarnished.

Motorists were traced who had been in the vicinity of Jedburgh at the material time and had taken the road to Hexham. Not one of them had seen such a man as Evelyn Foster had described.

She had said that her assailant told her that the people who gave him the lift to Elishaw had treated him to tea in Jedburgh. The police visited every café, hotel, farmhouse and inn for miles around. No one at any of them remembered serving such a party.

Surely John Scott, the barman at the Percy Arms, where the man in the bowler had gone for a drink while Evelyn went off to refuel her car, would recall the stranger. He did not. He said that no stranger had come into the Percy Arms that Tuesday evening.

It was now that an imp of perverseness seems to have got into the police mind. It was only a short step from failing to find an "invisible assassin" to denying his existence. And that, by the time the inquest on Evelyn Foster took place, seems to have been the position that the thwarted Northumberland constabulary had taken up.

The coroner, Mr Phillip Dodds, and his jury met at Otterburn's War Memorial Hall, where, only a few short weeks before, Evelyn Foster had attended a Boxing Night dance. A withered bunch of mistletoe still hung above the coroner's black-draped table.

It did not take long for those present to see the way things were being officially directed. Incredibly, the suggestion, discreetly canvassed, was that Evelyn Foster had deliberately set fire to herself.

It was monstrous. A crying shame. But with slow, inexorable dignity, the discreetly muffled nod, wink, nudge campaign got under way.

Up stepped dignified Professor Stuart McDonald, occupant of the Chair of Pathology at the Medical College of Newcastle. He had, he said, examined the dead girl's body. No, no indication of her having been raped. No, no sign of any blow to the head or face sufficiently violent to have stunned her. And, yes, the distribution of the burns on her body suggested to him that she had been sitting down during the period of her incineration.

The medicine man of the north was followed by the down-to-earth machine man, who preferred an intimidating display of motor-mechanic expertise to substantiate the notion that the car had been driven slowly off the road *before* the fire had been deliberately started by the sprinkling of petrol from a can at the rear of the car.

Certainly the coroner made no bones about his personal belief. Delivering from under the shrunken mistletoe his kiss of death to the reputation of the dead girl, he said: "My opinion, I must say, is that I do not think there is sufficient evidence to say that these burns were caused by another person."

[OT]TERGAPS TRAGEDY.

[F]UNERAL OF GIRL VICTIM IN VILLAGE CHURCHYARD.

COUNTRYSIDE'S TRIBUTES.

POLICE STILL INQUIRING AFTER MYSTERY

HUNDREDS OF MOURNERS.

WOMAN ELECTROCUTED.

Shock from Electric Heater.

TRAGIC AFFAIR AT SHIREMOOR HILL

Mother of 8 Children.

PRINCESS ROYAL'S FUNERAL.

EXTRAORDINARY VEHICULAR SPEED.

"AMAZED" LEADERS

Mr Graham Calls Answer

INTERPRETATION QUESTION

BURIAL OF VICTIM OF OTTERBURN TRAGEDY.

How, then, might they have been caused?

Like those of judges, coroners' utterances are privileged.

Did the girl, he asked, set fire to the car herself, and in so doing obtain the burns accidentally?

Might it have been to obtain money from the insurance?

Or – another scurrilous alternative – "There are cases where a person becomes obsessed, for some inexplicable reason, with the idea either of gaining notoriety or of doing something abnormal."

To all intents and purposes the coroner was practically directing the jury to find, one way or another, that Evelyn Foster had fired the car herself.

One is tempted to ask: what is the coefficient of expansion of brass neck!

In fact, there was absolutely nothing to suggest that Evelyn Foster had done anything of the kind. She had stood in no financial need – indeed, she left quite a substantial sum of money – and her parents testified that she had no worries of any sort.

One has the uneasy feeling that the police had decided to make the dead girl the scapegoat for their own clumsy-booted inefficiency.

They had failed to find the man in the bowler . . . so there wasn't one.

It was as simple – and crude – as that.

The jury would have none of it. They – the vicar who had buried her, the sub-postmaster, the landlord of the Percy Arms, men who had known her all her short life – utterly rejected officialdom's face-saving verdict.

"Wilful murder against some person or persons unknown," they declared stolidly.

"I suppose you mean that somebody deliberately poured petrol over her and set her on fire?" observed the coroner bleakly.

"Yes, we do," came the emphatic reply.

Evelyn Foster had been resoundingly vindicated. The villagers greeted the verdict with cheers.

The case of the burning girl had been concluded – but not resolved.

The mystery is still alive. So many questions remain glowing unanswered in the grey moorland air.

Of course, there have been theories. But only one seems worthy of a second – and perhaps a third and a fourth – thought. It is that advanced by the crime historian Jonathan Goodman.[1]

To give ear to Mr Goodman's advocacy, we must turn aside from Northumberland's pikes and fells, travel a hundred or so miles south-easterly, and two years forward in time, and attend to another fire-lit tale of murder. The setting is a lonely farmhouse on the Yorkshire moors. The story, old as the hills of Millstone Grit enfolding its puppet actors, is a timeless one of infidelity and intrigue; a Chatterley tale of love to hatred turned between a groom and his master's lovely, loose, compliant lady.

The groom, Ernest Brown, thirty-one-year-old widower, father of one child, had come to work for Frederick Ellison Morton in 1929.

Morton, although only twenty-four, had established himself in an exceedingly good way of business. He was the managing director and sole controller of a prospering firm of cattle factors. He was a relatively rich man, well able to indulge a fancy for fine hunter horseflesh. His wife Dorothy, about his own age, was an attractive, vigorous, vital young woman, possessed of that charm of manner which so often accompanies careful nurturing and ensues upon education at a well-known and superior girls' school. She was a keen horsewoman, and it was not only to tend the horses, but largely so that his wife should have someone to ride out with on those very numerous occasions when he was too busy earning everyone's fodder to keep her company, that Morton had taken Brown on. A fine specimen of a man – big, strong, seductively deep-tanned and surprisingly well-spoken – the new groom made a most favourable impression.

Predictably, the relationship soon developed into a sexual one. But rapidly as it had blossomed, so – on Dorothy Morton's side, at least – did it wither.

And that withering brought with it dead husks of bitterness and resentment. His bitterness because the lady of the house

1. In *The Burning of Evelyn Foster*, David & Charles, Newton Abbot, 1977; Headline, London, 1988.

had made it peremptorily obvious that her desires could dispense with his services. Her resentment that the over-zealous groom, refusing to take no for an answer, should continue to force his no longer welcome servicings upon her.

What may be termed the illicit honeymoon had lasted a star-blinded twelve-month. By 1930's end, those mad-shot stars were back in their spheres. It was only the spur of the black-mail threat to make a clean breast of all to Mr Morton that kept the reluctant lady a dancer to the groom's crude pipings.

Mrs Morton, who was, in the quaint argot of the period, a "flapper", did most perilously contrive a number of contem-poraneous side-saddle jaunts, despite Brown's uncomfortably tight reigning.

In 1931 Dorothy Morton bore her husband's child, and a nurse-companion, Ann Houseman, joined the staff.

Undeterred by Mrs Morton's translation into motherhood, Brown continued after her in full cry. He became increasingly threatening. She became increasingly frightened. Growing ever more surly, and with it more bullying and brutal, the emotionally frustrated Brown kept doggedly pressing his physical claims. He kept nourished, too, a terrible jealousy. All his mistress's movements were henceforth scrutinized and catechized.

It was early in 1933 that the Mortons moved from their home near Huddersfield to an isolated farm, Saxton Grange, Saxton, situated four miles south of Tadcaster, way beyond the hamlet of Towton. Ernest Brown and Ann Houseman went with them.

In June 1933 it seemed as if Dorothy Morton might at last be able to throw off the yoke of Brown's "moral" restraint; find herself free to go her own sweet waywardly free way. After an altercation with the boss, as he always called Mr Morton, over the order to mow a lawn – which job he considered *lèse-majesté* for a groom – Brown packed his slender baggage, quit the wooden hut near the farmhouse which had been his allocated quarters, and stomped angrily away into the sunset.

But Dorothy Morton was not really surprised (disappointed, yes – dreadfully – but not surprised) when, a matter of mere days later, Brown reappeared in her husband's business absence and terrorized her into telephoning Mr Morton and trying to persuade him to reinstate the bolshie groom. This he would under no circumstances, and in response to no amount of desperate wifely cajolement, assent to doing. What he would – and did – do, was take Brown back in the much humbler position of lawn-mowing odd-job man. Filled with spite and *malum*, Brown nonetheless accepted this lacklustre post.

While paying (bitten) lip-service to "the boss", the grievously slighted Brown snarled behind his back prognostications and promises of evil to come.

"I can wreck this place and I shall do it," he raved to any farmworker who would listen to his talk. Such was his hatred that you could almost *see* it twisting out of him.

Tuesday, 5 September 1933, was the day the hate exploded.

The boss had driven off on business to Oldham in his Chrysler Saloon. His other car, an Essex (oddly enough, practically identical with the Hudson Super-Six in which Evelyn Foster had been incinerated) remained in the garage.

Brown, too, was away most of the day with the horse-box.

It was the groom who got back to Saxton Grange first. He came crunching up the gravelled drive at half-past eight. Dorothy Morton happened to be in the yard. He asked her if the boss was back. She told him no. Then he asked her how she had spent the day. She said that she had gone swimming in the river at Wetherby. Who with? When she mentioned the name of her companion – a man whom Brown jealously regarded as a rival – everything within him suddenly erupted in a boiling lava stream of anger and, the flood of hot pressure building beyond endurance, his arm chopped out like an automaton's, knocking her to the ground.

"I tried to shout for help. He tried to push me into the horse-box," she was later to tell the densely-packed little magistrates' court of the old-world Yorkshire market-town of Sherburn-in-Elmet, and repeat to the leathery ear and fish-cold eye of Mr Justice Humphreys at the West Riding Autumn Assize.

Ann Houseman appeared. Brown, who had been edging Mrs Morton into the barn, and, according to her, trying with his powerful thumbs to strangle her, quickly pushed her aside. He loped moodily away.

Now there would be a lulling time.

The women went into the house. One to sew. One to make jam.

A sudden sharp explosion. A rattle of falling pellets outside the kitchen window. Both women, startled, jumped nearly out of their skins.

Brown came in. Funny sort of expression on his face. "Been shooting at a rat over by the cowshed," he said curtly. Then sidled out into the dusk again.

At 9.45 the telephone rang. Ann Houseman made her way to the drawing-room to answer it. Passing through the hall, she came upon Brown. He was just standing there, silently, still as a statue, sort of furtive and sly. It gave her quite a turn.

The telephone call was for Mr Morton, from someone in Carlisle. She told him that the Master was still out, and advised him to have another try in about a quarter of an hour's time. But the telephone never rang again that night – and, as we shall see, for a very good reason.

Ann Houseman rejoined Mrs Morton in the kitchen. They had not been together there more than a few minutes when Brown came in again. He crossed to the knife-drawer, took a knife from it, and, muttering something about cutting the head-rope from a loose horse, went swiftly out into the yard. As was subsequently proved, it was shortly afterwards that the telephone went dead. The caller from Carlisle rang back at ten o'clock. The line was out.

Brown returned to the kitchen. He was carrying a shotgun under his arm.

"You go out," he told Ann Houseman. "I want to talk to Mrs Morton." But the girl refused to leave. He then proceeded to clean the gun – taking out two cartridges.

After a little while, the women said goodnight to him. Mrs Morton went to her bedroom and the nurse to hers, where the child also slept. Neither of them undressed. Some sort of instinctual warning system must have clicked on to red-alert. They waited in separate silences.

Then . . . at 11.30 p.m. . . . relief. The sound of a motor engine. A car coming along the road to the house. They both ran down to the hall, expecting to see the welcome familiar figure of Mr Morton. Footsteps. The front-door creaked open. They moved forward in greeting. But it was Brown. "The boss has been in and gone out again," he said.

The women's night of terror had begun.

The trickle of unease which had been steadily mounting spilt over now into a spreading wash of fear. Realizing the absolute necessity to dissimulate – to repair, as it were, the emotional dam-walls – the women determinedly engaged Brown in inconsequential chatter, going at it full-spate until midnight, when he left them, ostensibly to go to his bed.

Once again they went unhappily upstairs. Silent and apprehensive they waited, every sense at peak, nerves taut, aware of the little flutterings of individual veins and arteries, the sporadic tic of a strand of over-tensed muscle.

Mrs Morton locked herself in the bathroom. Ann Houseman had gone into her bedroom. Peeping cautiously out of the window, keeping a wary eye open for the menacing figure of Brown, she suddenly spotted him, moving across the yard, stealthily in and out of the shadows, padding, soft-footed, to the unlocked back door. Heart pounding, the blood singing in her ears, she flung open the bedroom door, and ran to join her mistress in the illusory safety of the barricaded bathroom.

Time ticked on. One o'clock. Half-past. Two o'clock. Half-past. Breath held, ears straining, they registered every infinitesimal sound, little cracks and creaks of wooden boards, that told them of the man creeping about in the secret darkness downstairs.

The sounds ceased. They let what seemed an infinite length of silent time slip like smooth black silk between their trembling fingers. Then tiptoed across the landing to the nurse's room.

At 3.30 a.m. the silence was suddenly and terrifyingly ripped apart by a series of strange staccato explosions and a sinister crackling sound, like the snapping of giant twigs. Dorothy Morton gently eased the curtains open and peered through the small slit. She was horrified to see the garage on the far side of the yard transformed into a roaring ball of fire. All other fears swamped by the red terror of the flames, the women tore downstairs to the telephone to raise the alarm. Picked up the receiver. It was totally lifeless.

Abandoning every pretence of fortitude and courage, succumbing to pure, unashamed panic, they rushed wildly back up the stairs. Mrs Morton snatched up her sleeping child . . . and out of the house they ran, under the crimson, enflamed night sky, into the cool, green sanctuary of the fields. Glancing

back from the safety-screen of a tall hedgerow, they saw
Brown blundering around in the yard, releasing the horses
from their loose-boxes, close by the garage. They could hear
the clatter of hooves above the roaring of the fire and the
spume-splash of the scattering gravel. Then, soaringly out of
control, scimitar-sharp above all the imbroglio of noise,
Brown's screaming, "Mrs Morton! Mrs Morton!", as he flitted
madly to and fro across the cobbles like a huge flame-lit bat.

Shuddering, they set off over the fields to find help. They
saw Brown pass them. He was a field's width away, on the
road, driving the horse-box.

It was not until nine o'clock the following morning that the
smoke and the red smother had sufficiently cleared for it to
be possible to approach close enough to get a proper look at
the steaming débris of the gutted garage. Brown had not been
far out when, earlier, staring at the crackling building, he had
remarked to the entrenched and embattled firemen, "By God,
if the boss is in there, he'll never be seen again." But he
should have added the word "alive" – because the boss, or
rather the charred and charcoal, cooked and twisted, headless,
limbless, fire-crisped cinder of a torso that had once been the
boss, was not only seen again, but rose up against him in
irrefutable accusation.

They dragged out the grotesquely distorted remains of the
two cars, ribbed metal skeletons a'flutter in the fresh morning
breeze with blackened pennons of flame-torn and tattered
upholstery. In the front passenger seat of the Chrysler was
something which bunches of keys and a once proudly unique
platinum-and-diamond wrought ring proclaimed to be
Frederick Ellison Morton.

In the normal way of such things, statements were taken by
the police.

The boss returned home about 11.30 p.m., volunteered
Brown. He was drunk. "The clever side out", was his jolly,
colloquial euphemism. He had put the car away, but told
Brown he intended to go out again. When he (Brown) said
goodnight to him, the boss was still sitting in the car in the
garage. Brown had then gone to bed. Could he suggest what
might have happened? Yes, regretfully, he could. The boss
was a heavy smoker. He knew for a fact that he had sometimes
slept in the car in the garage. Not difficult really to make a

reasonable guess, was it? Clever side out, he was likely racing the engine up, and back-firing started the blaze.

Brown had had his say. Now it was Morton's turn. He made his statement through the medium of one square inch of blackened skin.

A post-mortem established that Morton had been dead *before* his body was burnt. In one small fragment of charred flesh from the chest which had escaped the full fury of the flames, the pathologist found shotgun pellets and, indisputably indicative of a shot's having been fired at close range, a scrap of gun-wad embedded in it. Had the wound been just an inch or two higher, it would never have been discovered – the fire would have destroyed it. In the context of that all-consuming holocaust, it was the millionth chance which – as so significantly frequently seems to happen above the rational statistical level of chance expectancy – loaded the dice against the iniquitous.

"If ever Fate played a murderer a dirty trick, it did so here," was how Crown counsel, Mr C. N. Roberts, was to put it.

The post-mortem results were communicated to the police. Brown was immediately arrested.

The whilom groom bridled at the charge and planted a firm denial. But the pellets and gun-wad had told a plain forensic tale that brooked no sophistry of contradiction, and items of his apparel submitted to the Home Office analyst unequivocally ratified its burden, underlining it in blood – sanguineous spotting being demonstrably manifest upon clothes, boots, and on the shotgun itself.

This matter-of-fact evidence substantiated as strong a *prima facie* case of murder as the most doubting of jury Thomases might require.

The preliminary hearing at the magistrates' court drew standing-room-only audiences.

Brown, sporting a canary-coloured pullover, watched by his anxiously-scanning mother and sister, permitted no shadow of emotion to play across his set-rigid face.

Mrs Morton came centre-stage. Appetizing, athletic-looking, a thirty-year-old woman in her prime, she set off to advantage the make-believe propriety of a severely-tailored, dark grey costume, frivolously contradicted by an impudently blue and white spotted scarf – and, perched on short brown hair, wavy and carefully-tended as a well-mown lawn, a question-begging grey straw hat. Below it, a strong face, with bold hazel eyes that seemed to answer the question.

Yes, the crowded court decided, a very attractive, even beautiful, woman.

Nor did she, in front of that roomful of friends and neighbours, pussyfoot with her evidence. Somehow managing to sidestep brazenry, she made full confession of her erstwhile passion, and unfalteringly shouldered the onus of its guilt. She broke down. Nearly collapsed. Recovered her dented composure. Frank and unhesitant in the witness box, she made her *confessio amantis* and her *peccavi*. Clearly, the crowded public benches gave her their absolution.

She endured the dissection of the examination-in-chief.

"Did you resist his advances or succumb to them?"

"I did not resist them."

"After twelve months, did you turn away his advances?"

"Yes."

"How did he take it?"

"He did not like it. He became threatening and I was very frightened."

"Did you ever tell your husband anything about this?"

"No."

"Why?"

"I dare not. I was frightened."

And survived cross-examination.

"Can you tell me the date of the last occasion on which intimacy took place between you?"

"Willingly or unwillingly?"

"Either."

"About June of this year."

Her three-hour ordeal at long last over, Dorothy Morton left the box and went to sit with her father, who had accompanied her to the court. She was grateful for the breath-taking; but she was going to have to endure it all again when the case came up for trial before Mr Justice Humphreys in the Assize Court at Leeds Town Hall, on Monday, 11 December 1933.

Dressed now demure in widow's black, sole concession to ornament a modish black fur, she once again unfolded her tale of poignancy and passion. Eyes downcast she had been frightened of Brown. Eyes frank and open but even more so of her husband. Eyes lowered once more, contritely, admission: she had weakly chosen acquiescent intimacy rather than life-upheaving exposure. Her original romantic feelings for her attentive attendant groom underwent a total reversal. She no longer felt bridal in his urgent embrace. Love-making became an obscene pantomime, but, under the prick of his intimidation, the emotional motley *had* to go on. She did not pretend to be a "good" woman; merely a human one. Yes, yes, there had been men other than Brown admitted to her boudoir intimacies. No, not a good woman – but honest.

Humphreys did not see it quite like that. Wrinkling the judicial nose, he was to describe her as "on her own confession an immoral person", but, the habit of equity rising in his juridical bosom, he meticulously added, "you need not necessarily disbelieve her on that account." Then, another equitable stab, prod, or pang beneath the scarlet and ermine, a further codicil of conscience: "What is more important, however, is that she is an angry woman. She has admitted that she hated Brown."

Standing at attention in the dock, smartly dressed and handsomely sun-burned, answering his plea, Brown struck the trial judge as a man "apparently somewhat above his station in life, but with a queer temper".

The case against him, the prosecution theory, was that he had shot his master between nine and half-past that fatal Tuesday night. It was proved that Morton had left a public-house and been seen driving towards his home in the Chrysler at about nine o'clock. After shooting Morton in the garage, and worried that the sound of the shot might have been heard up at the farmhouse, Brown had, it was alleged, fired off a second shot at a pretended rat, in the cow-yard, close to the kitchen. Later, when he believed Mrs Morton and the nurse to be safely asleep, he had poured petrol over the dead man, splashed it around the garage, and put a light to the place. The evidence suggested that that would most probably have been at about 3.30 a.m..

The prosecution further averred that Brown had deliberately cut the telephone wire at Saxton Grange. He had, they said,

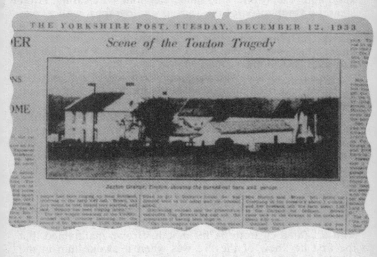

Scene of the Towton Tragedy

used for that purpose a white-handled game-knife which he had taken from the kitchen drawer.

Brown admitted taking a knife – a black-handled one – but said that it was to cut a dangling head-rope from a horse which had broken free; the job done, he had at once replaced the knife from where he had borrowed it.

An expert witness, Professor Frederick Tryhorn, Professor of Chemistry at Hull University College, testified that photographs had been taken showing the marks made by the severing instrument on the leaden casing of the cut telephone-wire magnified more than a hundred times. He had then photographed, under like magnification, the cutting edges of both the white-handled game-knife and the black-handled ordinary kitchen knife, which Brown claimed was the one that he had actualy taken from the drawer. The Professor had additionally photographed, under the same high magnification, the results of cuts made experimentally by himself with the white-handled knife upon a portion of the same telephone-wire casing. After a careful comparison of the various photographs, witness was confident in expressing the definite opinion that the Saxton Grange telephone-wire had been cut with the white-handled knife, which was the one which Mrs Morton was sure that she had seen Brown take.

Medical evidence was then called to the effect that the deceased had been shot some hours before the fire started, and had been killed not by the flames but by a gun.

Brown vigorously denied the prosecutor's scenario. But his defence was pitiful in its inadequacy – the evidentially unsupported hazarding of some innominate hypothetical stranger who, for some unspecified and seemingly unspecifiable reason, had shot Morton, and afterwards fetched the white-handled knife from the house and cut the telephone-wires. That was, of course, always provided that Mr Morton had not – as, indeed, Brown stated that he strongly believed that he *had* – caused the fire himself, by dropping drunkenly off to sleep with a lighted cigarette in his mouth. Brown maintained that the first he knew of the fire was when it awoke him in the middle of the night, and he rushed out to rescue the animals and give the alarm.

Back and forth, the life and death battle of tongues waged for the space of three days, the scales oscillating. And suddenly it was all over.

On Wednesday, 13 December, unlucky for some, Mr Justice Humphreys summed up conscientiously.

The jury, Yorkshire pudding-faced, filed out. They stirred their brains for seventy minutes. They returned with a verdict of Guilty.

The chaplain placed the black cap atop Mr Justice Humphreys's wig. The judge, expressing his agreement with the jury's finding, sentenced Ernest Brown to be hanged for what he called a "cruel and brutal murder".

Brown stood immovable and unflinching as a Millstone Grit boulder. Once – just once – as he turned and was being led below, he lifted his eyes to meet the hazel gaze of his sweet lady. Who shall guess what final message flashed between them?

Originally fixed for 1 February 1934, merry Christmas and happy New Year joyously intervening, the execution was stayed on 30 January, following information relating to some history of insanity, providentially discovered in the prisoner's family, being placed before the Home Secretary by the condemned man's solicitor.

Dr Norwood East, Medical Commissioner of His Majesty's Prisons, and Dr H. P. Foulerton, Medical Superintendent of Broadmoor Criminal Lunatic Asylum, were appointed to conduct an inquiry. Brown's "previous" revealed nothing of significance – two convictions for theft, six for being drunk and disorderly. The doctors conducted various tests, physical and psychiatric. They found no reason to interfere with the postponed sentence of the law taking its course. At Armley Gaol, Leeds, Brown was duly hanged, on 6 February 1934.

What possible linkage is there to be established between the homicidal Lothario of Saxton Grange and the pyromaniacal killer of Wolf's Nick – save, perhaps, that both victims were variantly accused of self-immolation? Jonathan Goodman has shrewdly espied persuasive connections.

Firstly, there is Evelyn Foster's description of her passenger's voice. She said that his accent was "like Tyneside – not broad Tyneside, but north-country". Ernest Brown, Mr Goodman points out, was born at Huddersfield and spent part of his childhood at Byker, an inner suburb of Newcastle upon-Tyne. That description, he believes, could well have applied to his accent.

Secondly, Evelyn Foster's murderer was "a bit of a knut". So was Brown – even the trial judge remarked his sartorial elegance.

Thirdly, both Evelyn Foster's murderer and Frederick Morton's incinerator knew how to drive a car – and that, in 1931, was very much a minority accomplishment, says Mr Goodman.

Fourthly, although Mr Goodman has not been able to ascertain whether or not Brown actually was away at a horse or cattle sale on 6 January 1931, it is, he says, a fact that it was part of his duties to attend such sales around the country on Mr Morton's behalf. And if it should so happen that he was, and if it should further happen that that sale took place anywhere near Jedburgh, then Brown's best route back to Huddersfield (where the Mortons were at that time living), would have been via Newcastle – the El Dorado of Evelyn Foster's killer.

Fifthly, there is the strange "evidence" of the execution shed. As Brown stood, pinioned and hooded, on the scaffold, the wan-faced chaplain breathed the gentlest professional hint that his soul might profit from a last confession. Back through the muffling white hood came either three words – they sounded like "ought to burn" – or was it perhaps *one* – "Otterburn"? The final truth, burked like the final

> *. . . prayer the hangman's snare*
> *Strangled into a scream*,

can never be known – but, observes Jonathan Goodman, "ought to burn" seems the least likely alternative.

It may be that, as Mr Goodman is the first to acknowledge, even taken together, these similarities, possibilities, potentialities, and portents, fall short of providing any credible basis for the proposition that Brown was a Janus killer, a north-and-south-facing double-murderer. All that can be advanced is the undeniable possibility that he *could* have been.

Whatever. . . . More than fifty snow-blown Januaries on, no solid clue has ever emerged as to the identity of the dapper little man in the bowler-hat who imported with him the lethal Will-o'-the-wisp flame. The man who materialized like some evil northland boggart out of the blackness of that long-ago winter's night, cruelly and senselessly incinerated a harmless young woman, and melted back into the shrouding darkness whence he came.

What manner of creature was he? A homicidal maniac? A wandering sexual psychopath? Was his name Smith, or Jones, or Brown? Did he ever, one wonders, kill again – differently, in another part of the forest?

Time has not bulked him out. He has remained what he was then: the invisible man – his entire existence, so far as we know it, encompassed in a few flame-lit hours in Otterburn. All, tangible, that remains to mark his terrible visitation, a black marble stone in the graveyard of St John's Church.

The Hudson Super-Six
Four-Door Sedan

The Hudson Super-Six
Custom Victoria

The Qualities Men Admire
Made Beautiful for Women

Men have pre-empted as altogether masculine the great qualities by which the Super-Sixes always led the values of the day; irrespective of the fact that dealers have always reported most Hudson and Essex purchases were made or influenced by women.

Their long, constantly improved leadership of chassis values, riding qualities, performance and operation smoothness is this year rounded out with the most beautiful, colorful and varied line of body designs we have ever presented—and to the greatest applause in our history.

The resources which achieved and led in mechanical

superiority have been brilliantly employed to create and lead a new mode of beauty, comfort and luxurious appointment.

Here is quality you can see in every detail of the finest cars Hudson and Essex ever built. Here is quality you can feel in the upholstery, in the wheel you handle and every fixture you touch.

Back of these cars stands one of the oldest and strongest automobile manufacturers, whose 19 years of constant growth reflects its alert leadership; and a dealer organization whose pride it is to make Hudson-Essex service as outstanding as the cars themselves.

The Judge's Black Cadillac

Albert Borowitz

CLEVELAND'S DEATH CORNER, the intersection of East 9th Street and Hamilton Avenue, no longer exists. Lost in the Erieview complex, the locale of the Kagy murder can be summoned up only by the most imaginative mind's eye.

The killing took place with startling suddenness shortly after midnight on Saturday, 8 May 1920. A black Cadillac touring car drove up East 9th Street towards Lake Erie and stopped at the corner of Hamilton. A number of passers-by saw three men get out of the car and heard words of argument. A shot was fired, and one of the men staggered away and fell in the doorway of a nearby garage. The two other men vanished in different directions, abandoning the Cadillac at the murder-scene.

The police quickly identified the car as belonging to William H. McGannon, first chief justice of Cleveland's Municipal Court and expected to be the next Democratic candidate for mayor. A familiar figure to Clevelanders, McGannon – about six feet tall and 250 pounds, a fashionable dresser credited with introducing the "Chesterfield" overcoat to his city – was recognized downtown shortly after the shooting; Detectives Burkhardt and Skala passed him in front of the lamented Weber's Café that used to stand on Superior Avenue near Public Square.

The victim was rushed to Lakeside Hospital, where he lingered in great pain until his death on 23 May. He was an automobile dealer and mechanic named Harold Kagy. From the moment the police discovered him crumpled in the garage entrance until his final statement shortly before his death, Kagy steadfastly maintained that he had been shot by another passenger in the Cadillac, John Joyce, a professional bondsman and saloonkeeper, who had a few days before the murder been arrested on a Prohibition charge. Kagy was extremely reluctant to talk about the third passenger in the car, who he admitted had been his good friend Judge McGannon; however, his two brothers, who heard his last words, understood him to say that the judge had left the car at 9th and Euclid before it proceeded further north to Hamilton.

The conflicting narratives of Kagy, Joyce and McGannon became the subject of three murder trials and a perjury prosecution. These court proceedings did little to resolve the bewildering variances in the three companions' accounts of the crime and of the events that preceded it.

In his final statement, made under oath in the presence of his brothers but excluded from evidence at the trials on the ground that it was not a dying declaration, Kagy said that after McGannon had left the car, the following events transpired:

> Joyce asked me to take him to a place near Hamilton Avenue NE and East 9th Street. When we got there and got out of the car, he asked to be taken somewhere else. When I told him it was time to put the car in the garage and that I couldn't take him any further, he said, "Well, I have a way of making people do what I want."

Johnny Joyce had a very different version of the night's occurrences, though for a long time he appeared to share Kagy's unwillingness to implicate Judge McGannon. In June 1920, Joyce reportedly told the prosecutor that the shooting had resulted from a quarrel over a stolen automobile. A man he did not name had drawn a revolver and aimed it at Joyce, saying, "I'll fix you." Johnny turned, and as he did so, the bullet passed him and struck Kagy in the back. The car-theft story had a short life; when Joyce faced murder charges in the light of Kagy's repeated accusations, he pointed the finger more accurately in the judge's direction. His ultimate version of the tragedy was as follows:

At about ten o'clock on Friday night, Joyce dropped in at Ferguson's at Euclid Avenue and Coltman Road. (Since this was Prohibition, the *Cleveland Plain Dealer* politely described the premises as a "former saloon".) At about eleven, Judge McGannon came in with Harold Kagy, to whom Joyce claimed McGannon introduced him for the first time. The entire party was under the influence of liquor – Joyce the most intoxicated and Kagy the least. The judge asked Joyce to join them in a ride downtown. Kagy took the wheel; McGannon was at his side and Joyce sat in the rear. At University Circle, they stopped the car and each took another drink from the bottle they were carrying. At East 79th Street, the car stopped again and the trio finished the contents of the quart and threw the bottle on to the street. When the car reached Euclid and East 9th Street, Kagy turned north to Hamilton. Joyce was asleep most of the time, but on the way downtown he overheard McGannon and Kagy quarrelling about money.

When Joyce got out of the car, he felt ill and leaned against a lamp-post as if to vomit. As he stood there, Kagy and McGannon resumed their quarrel, and Joyce and other witnesses standing by heard remarks such as "I'll stand for nothing like that," and "What did you do with the money?" Shortly afterwards, while Joyce was still slumped against the lamp-post, a shot was fired. He stumbled away from the scene and eventually slept off his drunkenness in his office at 718 Superior Avenue.

Judge McGannon (whom the *Plain Dealer*, anticipating Graham Greene and Orson Welles, delighted in referring to as "the third man") was first questioned by the police at his home about two hours after the shooting. He told Captain Charles Sterling and the other detectives who had roused him and his wife from sleep – and he always insisted thereafter – that he had left the car before it arrived at Death Corner. He said that he had left City Hall a little after 4.00 p.m. on Friday and met Kagy at Euclid Avenue and East 55th Street about 8.00 p.m. Kagy was driving the judge's Cadillac, which he had taken to repair, and the two men tested it out by driving along Lake Shore Boulevard to the north-eastern suburb of Willoughby. On the way back they stopped, at Kagy's suggestion, at a restaurant, and there the judge took "a mouthful or two of brandy". They had nothing further to drink on the drive into town, and soft drinks were their only refreshments at Ferguson's – where they encountered Johnny Joyce, who appeared to the judge to be intoxicated. McGannon said that Johnny had stood with his back to the desk in Ferguson's office and that a revolver that the judge had seen on the desk as he observed Joyce from the doorway had disappeared when he looked again a few minutes later.

McGannon denied that there had been any stops for drinking bouts during the subsequent drive downtown, and tried to put an innocent light on the quarrels about money that Joyce claimed to have overheard. When they arrived at the corner of Euclid Avenue and East 9th Street, he had awakened Joyce to tell him that this was as far as they were going. Here the judge had offered Kagy money – $11 for repairs to the car – but the friendly mechanic had refused to accept anything.

The judge said good-night to Kagy and Joyce at East 9th Street and walked towards Public Square. At Vincent Avenue he turned to look back and saw the car still standing where he had left it. He strolled on to Superior Avenue and turned west to the Square, where he boarded a Euclid Avenue streetcar and went home. When he was asked why he had walked to Public Square to catch a Euclid streetcar when he was already on Euclid Avenue, the judge offered the explanation that he would not have been able to find a seat by the time the streetcar reached East 9th Street. Cleveland must have been a livelier place on weekend nights in 1920.

Judge McGannon's claim to have left the Cadillac before it arrived at Death Corner conflicted with the statements of several eye-witnesses who identified him as the bulky third man who fled the murder-scene. The witnesses included two policemen, a bowling-alley scorekeeper, and a Canadian war-veteran who recognized McGannon from having seen him at City Hall. These informants put the judge's candour in doubt early in the investigation, but Kagy's accusations and the judge's fine civic reputation combined to make Johnny Joyce the prime suspect.

In November 1920, Joyce was brought to trial for the murder of Kagy and was acquitted. Nine days later, the grand jury indicted Judge McGannon for second-degree murder. Ordinarily, justice is not well served by consecutive trials of two alternative and mutually exclusive suspects for the same crime, but in this case the prosecution had, or thought it had, a good reason: it seemed that the "third man" had a "second woman". She was a thirty-nine-year-old nurse named Mary Neely, who had known the judge for sixteen years. There was, of course, a good deal of speculation about their relationship; but neither the newspapers nor the police peered too closely,

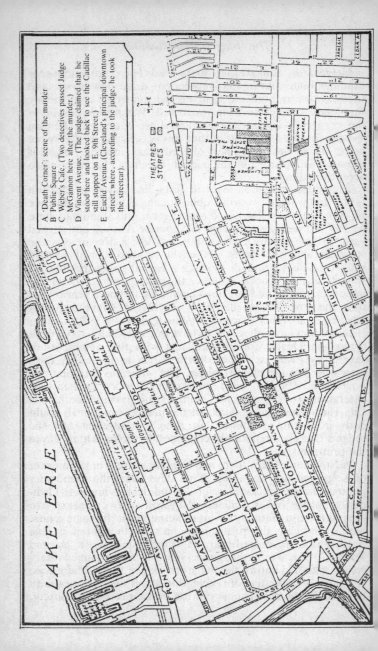

LAKE ERIE

A 'Death Corner': scene of the murder
B Public Square
C Weber's Cafe. (Two detectives passed Judge McGannon here after the murder.)
D Vincent Avenue. (The judge claimed that he stood here and looked back to see the Cadillac still stopped on E. 9th Street.)
E Euclid Avenue (Cleveland's principal downtown street, where, according to the judge, he took the streetcar).

THEATRES ▨▨
STORES ▤▤

and presiding Judge Maurice Bernon kept prosecution questioning under tight rein. Still, it was apparent that the witness's friendship with McGannon had had its ups and downs. For a year they had met every day, and then for several years about three times a week; then their meetings had been much less frequent until November 1919, when they had started seeing each other daily again. So far as one can glean from the trial reports, she had been spying on Judge McGannon, whom she suspected of some unspecified improper behaviour. She testified that on the morning of 7 May she saw Judge McGannon's car in front of an apartment house at East 85th Street and Hough Avenue. She watched the judge and Kagy come out of the house and drive away. Asked by Prosecutor Roland A. Baskin what she did next, she gave the remarkable answer that she telephoned Mrs McGannon to describe what she had seen and then "went downtown to report to the Bar Association". Late that night, she was riding on a Euclid Avenue streetcar near East 9th Street and thought she recognized the judge's Cadillac. She got off hurriedly as the Cadillac turned the corner at East 9th, and followed it up the street. Standing two short blocks away from Hamilton Avenue, she saw the judge and Kagy help someone out of the car. The judge and Kagy stood there talking for about twenty minutes. Miss Neely's next words caused quite a stir in the courtroom:

"I observed Kagy start to walk away. As he turned, I saw McGannon pull something out of his pocket, and simultaneously I saw a shot fired. Kagy pitched forward. The judge then crossed East 9th Street and went down Hamilton Avenue. He was trying to put something in his pocket. I don't know what it was."

Miss Neely claimed that she had informed the judge that she had seen the shooting and had exhorted him repeatedly to tell the police that it was an accident. She recalled having said to him: "I know you were all drunk. . . . You are making yourself ridiculous in the eyes of the public by making two or three statements." McGannon, however, had rejected her advice on the ground that it was too late to change his story. He had had a better idea of his own. During a car-ride in November, just before his trial, he had told her that he was trying to get someone to say that he had seen him leave the Cadillac at East 9th and Euclid. After he heard that Mary was talking to the police and might appear before the grand jury, he had offered her "five new $100 bills" for favourable testimony.

Miss Neely's testimony was counterbalanced by a parade of defence witnesses who supported McGannon's alibi; and a taxi-driver testified that he had driven Miss Neely and two other women near the outskirts of the city at the time of the shooting. It is no wonder that the jury, faced with this conflicting evidence, failed to reach a verdict. Still deadlocked after fifty-three ballots, they were discharged on New Year's Eve.

Five days after the first McGannon trial, the Cleveland Foundation, "spurred on by recent outrages of murder and robbery which police are apparently unable to check," announced that it would undertake a survey of the administration of criminal justice in Cleveland under the direction of two luminaries of Harvard Law School, Dean Roscoe Pound and Professor (later United States Supreme Court Associate Justice) Felix Frankfurter. The second trial and its aftermath amply proved that the survey was timely. Mary Neely, asked at the re-trial whether she saw Judge McGannon on or about 7 May, stated: "I refuse to answer because, in doing so, I might disgrace or incriminate myself – Judge McGannon is not guilty of the murder of Harold Kagy." This turn of events contributed to the jury's acquittal of McGannon.

However, the prosecution was not prepared to let the matter rest. Perjury indictments were brought against McGannon, Mary Neely, and a large number of witnesses for the judge and for John Joyce. McGannon was indicted for perjury in testifying that he had left the automobile at Euclid Avenue, and indictments were also brought against the taxi-driver who had claimed to have transported Miss Neely elsewhere on the murder-night and against six of the judge's alibi-witnesses. McGannon was convicted of perjury – also of conspiracy with two former reporters of the *Cleveland News* to induce Miss Neely to change her testimony. The star witness in the judge's perjury trial was once again Mary Neely. Under the shadow of her own perjury indictment, she once again changed her story, repeating her original testimony that she had seen the judge shoot Kagy. Pressed by Judge Florence Allen to explain her inconsistent statement at McGannon's second murder-trial, Mary revealed that she was a woman scorned. She had promised her silence in exchange for McGannon's bribery-money and his promise "to give up a certain friend, to be more attentive to his wife, to go to church, and to be a better man". The reference to the judge's other "friend" seemed to cast new light on McGannon's rendezvous at the apartment on East 85th Street on the day of the murder.

Judge Florence Allen sentenced McGannon to a term of from one to ten years in the Ohio Penitentiary on the perjury indictment. As he turned to leave the courtroom, he cried out:

> As there is a Jesus Christ in Heaven, he will make these people suffer as I have suffered. He will torture them and punish them as I have been punished. If they don't suffer as I have suffered, then there is no God.

In January 1924, when McGannon had served nineteen months in the penitentiary, the parole board freed him. The release was granted on the recommendation of the prison physician, who advised the board that the judge was suffering from a grave case of diabetes. McGannon came back to Cleveland but could not return to the practice of law, having been disbarred because of his conviction. With his wife, who had stood by him through his tribulations, he moved to Chicago, where he found a job as a clerk in a law firm. In 1928, he died of a heart-attack while boarding a streetcar.

In crime history, as in human affairs generally, it is indeed an ill wind that blows no good. The sordid murder of Harold Kagy, and the insight it gave that a leading judge was not above perjury, obstruction of justice, and perhaps homicide as well, was the catalyst for the Cleveland Foundation's trail-blazing study of the administration of urban justice.

Woman of Evil

Ian Forbes[1]

I WAS WRITING when she entered the office and I did not look up. She accepted the chair a detective placed alongside me, and slowly I turned to face her.

Crime reporters had said she was quite a siren. I couldn't fault that judgment. She was tall and blonde and slender. She wore an elegant grey costume, silk stockings on her long legs, and she had an air of easy confidence, as if she knew what effect she had on men and enjoyed every bit of it.

In different circumstances I would have been the first to admit that this twenty-three-year-old girl would have been a very attractive companion, but I knew I was looking at the most evil woman it was my misfortune to meet in my thirty-odd years as a policeman – blonde, bouffant-haired Valerie (Kim) Newell. Shrewd, cold, calculating and hard, she had been chased by men from the time she was little more than a child and I was to discover that she had manipulated two of them like puppets on a string.

They had responded to a woman who was the architect of four separate plans to murder an innocent wife. Plan four had been carried out and the woman who had been in Kim Newell's way was dead.

She could not meet my gaze as I said quietly, "I understand you told Norman Lucas, the *Sunday Mirror*'s chief crime reporter, that you would like to see the man from the Yard. . . ."

We talked for only twenty minutes. She didn't know then that I was playing a cat-and-mouse game, and was not yet ready to pounce. I had not completely penetrated the web of

1. Ex-Deputy Assistant Commissioner, Scotland Yard (a detective superintendent in 1967).

intrigue and deception this she-devil had woven around the two men she had blackmailed into murder. I had no evidence against her and she offered no help, but I was more than satisfied that she was mixed up in this killing – indeed, that she was the key to the whole business.

I began pulling aside the strands of the web on 7 March 1967, when I halted the funeral of Mrs June Serina Cook, the schoolmistress wife of a draughtsman, Raymond Sidney Cook. Gradually I uncovered a stranger-than-fiction story of how four lives had become enmeshed – a story that was to end in brutal death for one and sentences of life imprisonment for the other three. When recalling this crime, I have often said it had all the ingredients of a typical Agatha Christie whodunit – sex, greed, blackmail, violence – and the opening scene might well have been set by that great writer.

It was a fine moonlit night on 2 March 1967, when Robin Franklin, a Reading fireman, left the Highwayman public house at Hook End with his friend, Colin Pinfield, of Peppard Road, Reading, to drive the few miles home. Their route took them along a narrow, winding lane between Hook End and Peppard, Oxfordshire, and as they were driving through lonely Rumerhedge Wood they saw a blue Ford Cortina parked on a bend in the road. The car had no driver, its boot was open and the sidelights were on.

As Franklin edged past the car to negotiate the bend, his headlights picked up a red Morris Mini half off the road, its bonnet about a foot away from the trunk of a large tree. Lying on the ground beside the vehicle, with her head slightly raised, was a woman, her face covered with blood. Franklin stopped his car, jumped out and ran towards the Mini. He then noticed a man crouching over the woman.

"Has an ambulance been called?" asked Franklin. The man, without raising his head, replied, "No, it hasn't," and added that there was someone else in the car. Pinfield left the scene to telephone for an ambulance and Franklin went round to the other side of the Mini. There was a man slumped forward in the passenger seat. He appeared to be uninjured, but kept saying he felt sick. He made an effort to get out of the car, but Franklin pushed him back and told him to stay where he was. While Franklin was dealing with the passenger, he heard

the other man say, "I'll go to my car and get some towels."
The man walked to the Cortina. Franklin heard the boot
and car door slam and the engine starting, and then, to his
astonishment, he saw the Cortina moving quickly away in the
direction of Hook End.

Franklin did what he could for the injured woman. The man
inside the car was groaning and asking, "What's happened?-
Where am I?" He then appeared to go to sleep.

When the ambulance arrived, he got out of the car and
walked towards the vehicle without assistance, although he
seemed dazed and fell from the seat of the ambulance during
the journey to Battle Hospital, Reading. The woman, who
was his wife, was obviously seriously hurt. She died in hospital
from terrible head injuries shortly after midnight.

After their admission to hospital, the man in the Mini, Mr
Raymond Cook – who had only a small abrasion on one knee
– was told by the duty casualty officer, Dr Atul Garrud, that
his wife's chances of survival were remote. Cook put his head
in his hands and said "Oh dear", but showed no other
emotional reaction. Asked if he could remember how the
accident occurred, Cook replied, "I don't know how it
happened."

I have always had a great respect for the copper on the beat,
and it was the highly intelligent PC Stephen (appropriately
named) Sherlock, the twenty-six-year-old village bobby at
Nettlebed, near Henley-on-Thames, Oxfordshire, who was
first suspicious about the crash. It was as a result of his initial
doubts that this case developed from what could have been
recorded as a normal fatal accident into a full-scale murder
inquiry.

He was the first officer to arrive at the scene, and he noticed
that the Mini, index number 4499 DP, appeared to have run
off the road and collided with a tree after failing to negotiate
a sharp left-hand bend. It soon became clear to him, however,
from the position of the vehicle, that it had turned across the
offside of the road after passing the apex of the bend rather
than having run out of road – in other words, it looked as if
the car had negotiated the bend and then been steered into
the tree.

Sherlock found that there was only minor damage to the
car. The windscreen was intact, and he felt sure that, although

there was a lot of blood on the driver's side of the vehicle, the injuries could only be slight in view of the trivial impact between car and tree. He was amazed, when he reached Battle Hospital, to find that Mrs Cook was dead, and even more astonished when he was told that her injuries had probably been caused by her being flung headlong through the windscreen.

The young officer questioned Raymond Cook, but could get no sense from him. Shortly after Mrs Cook died, Sherlock drove Cook home in a police car. As they left the hospital, he asked Cook if he could direct him to his home at Farley View, Spencer's Wood, Reading, as Sherlock was unfamiliar with that area. In view of Cook's apparently confused condition and previous mumbling incoherence, the officer was not very optimistic about help from him. He was therefore puzzled when Cook gave clear and concise directions throughout the journey. It was only when Sherlock put any questions relating to the accident to Cook that the man became vague, and by the time they reached his home, Sherlock was convinced that he had been putting on an act. As soon as he had seen Cook into bed, the officer sent a message to County Police Headquarters saying that he was not satisfied with the circumstances of the accident, and requesting the attendance of a scenes-of-crime officer (a type of specialist recently introduced).

Later that morning he returned to Rumerhedge Wood with Detective Sergeant John McMiken, a police photographer, and found blood on the road seventy yards from the Mini.

Police Sergeant Donald Franklin, of Oxfordshire Constabulary traffic department, found only minor damage to the Mini when he examined it. He concluded that with steering, brakes and tyres in good condition, there was nothing to make the car unroadworthy. He thought the damage was consistent with impact at a speed of about ten miles an hour.

A pathologist, Dr Derek Barrowcliff, reported that Mrs Cook had died of multiple head injuries. Her neck was broken and she had nine scalp wounds. There was no glass or gravel in the wounds, and Dr Barrowcliff did not believe they had been caused in a car crash. He concluded that the woman had not been in the driving seat at the time the wounds were inflicted; the characteristics of the broken neck indicated that she had been on her knees, her neck forced downwards.

The Cooks' Morris Mini

Dr Barrowcliff's opinion was that four of the head wounds had been incurred at about the same time, indicating a repetitive action on the part of an attacker. An area of bruising over the crown of the head was such as would have occurred if her attacker had grasped her hair. There were fingernail marks on the forehead and in the right eye which could have been caused if her head had been held by her attacker's right hand while he was standing above and behind her.

When Sherlock called at Farley View on 3 March, the day after the crash, he found that Raymond Cook had recovered from his apparent confusion. Cook was able to make a statement, which he later elaborated in an interview with Detective Inspector Tony Insell of Henley.

He said that he and his wife had had a meal and some drinks at the George Hotel, Pangbourne, and that he was driving when they left the hotel shortly before ten o'clock in the evening. They had agreed to return home via Whitchurch, Woodcote and Peppard "for a change of scenery" although it was not the most direct route. He began to feel sick just after they passed the Highwayman public house, and he left the car to get a breath of air. His wife said she was feeling fine, and he accepted her offer to take over the driving.

"I remember coming to the junction where there was a signpost to Peppard," Cook stated. "We went along this road. I was feeling rather depressed and sick. I wasn't looking at the road and probably had my eyes shut. I suddenly heard my wife say 'Oh'. I looked up and saw headlights on full-beam in front of us. . . . I got the impression we were travelling at about thirty to forty miles per hour. . . . We seemed to veer to the left and I saw a tree loom up in front of us and felt a bump. I do not remember much else."

Cook added that he had found bloodstains on his coat and trousers after the accident, so he had taken the clothes to be cleaned. He had burned his bloodstained gloves in the kitchen-boiler at his home.

Accident? Detective Chief Inspector Arthur Wooldridge (Head of Reading CID) and Tony Insell had grave doubts. Scotland Yard was called, and I left London with Detective Sergeant Peter Hill on 7 March.

We arrived at Reading at eight o'clock that night, and Mr L. C. Dolby, Acting Chief Constable of Reading, introduced me to his team of detectives. It has always been my view that in cases like this, where a Scotland Yard murder-squad man goes into "foreign" territory, the best way to get to know the local officers and learn their opinions is to join them in a glass of beer. At my suggestion, we adjourned to the police club. It was during an informal chat there that I learned that arrangements had been made for June Cook to be cremated next day.

I put a stop to that. I had a strong feeling that the unfortunate woman's body was likely to be the subject of further examination. The funeral was cancelled, and the following day we started a full-scale murder inquiry – carried out with the smallest team of officers on any murder inquiry I have ever experienced. There were many pressures on the local police, but I had at my disposal a number of officers from Oxfordshire, plus Regional Crime Squad men from No. 5 region (based at Hillingdon, Maidenhead and Reading) and men of No. 6 Regional Crime Squad from Hampshire. We were small in

number but the men formed a grand team, willing and anxious
to bring matters to a successful conclusion.

When I examined Mrs Cook's body at the mortuary and
took a good look at the Mini, I could understand why Dr
Barrowcliff had expressed the opinion that her injuries could
not have been caused in the crash.

The car had two main centres of bloodstaining, one on the
steering column and the carpet below it, and the other around
the bottom of the driver's doorway. There were also bloodstains on the outside of the Mini. These stains and blood
splashes told us that the origin of some of the splashing must
have been in the area of the driver's door, at a level below
the dashboard-shelf. This meant that somehow Mrs Cook had
been forced downwards in the car to seat-level. Yet the impact,
no matter how slight, would have forced her forwards and
upwards.

Mr Brian Culliford, a principal scientific officer of the
Metropolitan Police Forensic Science Laboratory, who also
examined the Mini, gave us an unusual but most useful piece
of evidence. In the collision, a sloping "rib" just in front of
the driver's door had sprung out of position away from the
main bodywork of the car. Some blood splashes had over-
lapped the bodywork and the rib, but there were no splashes
on the strip exposed by the displacement of the rib. This
could only mean that the rib had become displaced *after* the
bloodstaining – the blood splashes first and the "accident"
second. Then, searching the scene, I found a small particle of
skull-bone in leaves and mould near the tree the Mini had hit.
None of it made sense.

Recalling Sergeant Franklin's estimate of the Mini's speed
of impact, I called the Ministry of Transport Accident
Research Unit and made another visit to Rumerhedge Wood
with Mr James Hobbs, an Experimental Officer.

We put a man and a woman of similar weight to the Cooks
in a Morris Mini saloon like the one used by the couple, and
let it run down the slight hill out of gear from the point at
which PC Sherlock had seen the bloodstains on the road.
Immediately before reaching the tree, the speed of the car
rose to 8 mph. This test was repeated four times: the speed
never exceeded 8 mph. If Mrs Cook had been dazzled by
oncoming lights, she would have removed her foot from the

accelerator and braked. Nevertheless, we carried out a second test, this time with the engine running, the car in first gear and the choke-control out – and the car made 9 mph.

Mr Hobbs, like Sergeant Franklin, considered that the Mini's damage would be consistent with an impact of under 10 mph. The injuries to the woman were inconsistent with a crash at that speed and could only be matched to a vehicle that would have ended up as a mass of tangled wreckage.

Cook, however, steadfastly maintained that his wife's death had been caused by the crash and that he could remember little apart from being blinded by oncoming headlights.

I looked into his background and made some interesting discoveries.

He was a giant of a man, six foot four inches tall, an ambling, boorish individual whose intellect was far below that of his wife. He gave the impression of being quiet and docile, but was subject to violent outbursts of temper. His parents-in-law, Mr and Mrs Henry Garrett, who lived next door to the Cooks at Farley View, told me of one instance.

Mrs Garrett had called at the Cooks' house late one night because she had heard a noise, and was greeted by Cook with "You bloody well keep out, you old cow." Mr Garrett then arrived on the scene and was roughly pushed aside by Cook. The Garrett's younger daughter, Cynthia, who was living with the Cooks, was pulled out of bed by Cook and pushed out of the house in her nightdress. He then snatched all the drawers from the furniture in Cynthia's room and tipped their contents on to the front doorstep. His final act of rage was to pick up a big Gurkha knife, run down the garden, and chop up a chicken-run owned by the Garretts.

But no one ever suggested that he had used violence towards his wife.

They were married in May 1958, seven months after her divorce from her first husband, a lieutenant in the Gurkha Regiment. Cook was twenty-three then, and she was thirty-two.

Five years after their marriage, Cook gave up his job as a draughtsman and became a student nurse at the nearby Borocourt Hospital for mentally retarded patients, earning only £750 a year – compared with his wife's salary of £1750. Actually, he was quite highly regarded at the hospital, but his work fell off shortly before his final examinations, and he failed them.

Apart from the disparity in their salaries, June Cook's financial position was far superior to that of her husband. She owned the house at Farley View – a gift from her father – and was also buying, on a mortgage, a house in High View Gardens, Upminster, Essex, where she had lived with her first husband before he left for America. This was let off in flats, and brought her an income of twelve pounds a week. At the time of her death, she had, in addition to cash in her current account, more than £1500 in a bank deposit account and stocks and shares worth about five thousand pounds.

Mrs Cook was apparently a rather self-opinionated woman, dogmatic in her views on teaching and religion, and inclined to be snobbish. She dominated her husband, but for some years the marriage had seemed reasonably happy and Cook was fond of their two children.

Quite early in the inquiry, we began to hear about Kim Newell, who claimed that she was a friend of both Raymond and June Cook. She made the front page in many of the national newspapers, and no one could deny that she photographed well. It soon became quite clear that she was Cook's mistress and that the affair had started shortly after she too had enrolled as a student nurse at Borocourt Hospital. Cook spent occasional nights with her at her flat in Reading, and they lived there together for a short while in 1966. It appeared that June Cook's behaviour towards her husband, coupled with the disparity in their ages, had led him to seek solace with this sex-siren who was as much his junior as he was his wife's.

He became completely infatuated with her. When the girl was dismissed from the hospital as unsuitable, Cook maintained her. After he had failed his final examinations, he was missing from duty for some days at the beginning of December 1966, and in the letter of resignation that the hospital then received, he gave his address as c/o Miss K. Newell at Sidmouth Street. He was unemployed until he went back to work as a draughtsman in February 1967.

When Mrs Cook heard of the affair between her husband and Kim Newell, she withdrew the balance of their joint current and deposit bank accounts, and all the cash went into

Kim Newell

an account in her sole name. On 20 December 1966 she relented and transferred the cash into another joint account with her husband. I found evidence of the "on and off" state of their marriage. In October 1966 Mrs Cook telephoned her solicitor, Mr George Burrows, requesting him to take out a summons against her husband for maintenance in respect of herself and children on the grounds of her husband's desertion. Three days later Mr Burrows received a letter from Mrs Cook in which she cancelled those instructions. Towards the end of November Mrs Cook again wrote to her solicitor to ask him to take out a maintenance summons, and a court hearing was fixed for 26 January 1967. Once more, however, the instructions were cancelled and the summons was withdrawn.

At one stage during this period, June Cook changed her will, cutting out her husband and making their two sons the sole beneficiaries. Later, when her husband returned to her – although he was still cohabiting with Kim Newell – she made another desperate attempt to save the marriage by making a further will in favour of her husband.

I found that on 4 November 1966 Raymond Cook had surrendered an insurance policy and received £677 6s. 7d. On the same day he opened a bank deposit account in his own name with £450, but by 2 March the following year, the day of the "accident", this account showed a nil balance. In spite of the fact that he had been drawing a salary from Borocourt Hospital during November, all he had left in his current account by the beginning of March was £35 18s. 8d.

There was no doubt that most of the money had been lavished on the girl Newell. On one occasion he gave her a blank cheque and told her to make it out for not more than £50. She drew £100, and he did not complain. Clearly he was besotted by this attractive and unprincipled young woman and was ready to spend every penny he had to keep her affections.

A motive for murder was becoming quite clear. Cook's need for cash became more desperate when Newell told him she was pregnant by him, and it was plain that he could only meet her further demands by making sure that his wife died while the will was in his favour.

On 17 March the inquest on Mrs Cook was opened and adjourned. I arrested Cook as he left the court and told him he would be charged with his wife's murder. Without emotion he said, "I understand." He never uttered another word about the killing until he was examined at his trial.

I could have closed my file on the Cook case at that point. A woman had been killed and I was sure I had caught the murderer. He had been arrested on good, substantial evidence . . . yet I was not satisfied. There were too many loose ends. Where was the weapon used to batter June Cook? Why had the Cortina driver vanished and, in spite of all appeals, failed to come forward?

Kim Newell, who had been fairly cautious in her remarks to newspapermen up to that point, became a good deal more loquacious after Cook's arrest. She could not understand why the police had arrested Raymond, why Scotland Yard should be interested in what was obviously an accident, and she told Norman Lucas: "I should very much like to meet this man from the Yard."

At that stage I thought it wouldn't be a bad idea if she *did* meet the man from the Yard. I was not much further forward when I sent her home after that twenty-minute interview, but I was told by Detective Sergeant Brian Sheridan, of No. 6 District Regional Crime Squad, who escorted her to her flat, that she was a very, very, frightened young woman. She had met the man from the Yard and she did not want to meet him again.

I didn't feel that the bumbling Cook had sufficient ingenuity to organize a tombola, let alone fake a murder to look like an accident – clumsy though it had been – but Kim Newell had the cunning. The more I thought about it, the more I thought that the operation had been two- or even three-handed, and I was willing to put a fiver on Newell being involved.

In the meantime, we were still looking for the owner of the Cortina. There was no reason to suspect that he was other than a passing motorist who had stopped to give assistance to the victim of "the accident" and had then decided, no doubt for his own private reasons, to disappear and disassociate himself from the whole business. It was essential, however, that he should be traced. Because the route through Rumerhedge Wood was a little-known one, it was thought that the driver must be a local man, and we began the tedious business of tracing all owners of blue Cortinas in the Borough of Reading, neighbouring districts in Berkshire, and the whole of the south Oxfordshire area.

It was a formidable task, made no easier by the fact that we were so very short of manpower. At just about this time, a schoolgirl was shot dead in a wood at Bracknell, Berkshire, and one of my colleagues, Detective Superintendent Frank Williams, was sent from Scotland Yard to handle the inquiry. We both needed men from the same police forces and had to share available officers. Then came the murder of two children in a disused gravel pit at Beenham, between Reading and Newbury. Another close colleague of mine, Detective Superintendent Bill Marchant, was put on to that case, and once again we had to share manpower. By this time I was down to about sixteen men on outside inquiries and four women to do the main bulk of the office work. Things were pretty grim and progress was slow.

You always need a little bit of luck on a murder investigation. Mine came in the shape of Angus MacDonald, a Reading painter and decorator. He walked into my office on 8 April and said, "I've come about the Cortina."

It seemed he had done some work at Borocourt Hospital, and while there had heard the common gossip of the affair between Cook and Newell. He had also seen Kim when visiting his mother, who lived next door to the girl in Sidmouth Street. Like many other young (and not so young) men in Reading, he regarded her as unusually attractive, although she was never more than a casual acquaintance.

On 2 March he had followed a blue Cortina over Reading Bridge just before 8 p.m. – two hours before the murder. It was driven by a man and there was a woman in the front passenger seat. When the Cortina halted at some traffic lights, MacDonald recognized the passenger as Kim Newell. The driver, however, was a stranger to him.

He then astonished me by adding, "The index number was 7711 FM." It is most unusual for motorists to remember the registration numbers of other vehicles, so I asked him how he was so sure.

"The figures 7711 were easy to remember," he replied. "As to the letters, I recollect saying to myself at the time, 'Fuck

me, another boy friend!' I'm quite sure of the number and I'm
certain the passenger was Kim Newell."

It was not surprising that we had failed to trace the blue
Cortina in our local inquiries. The vehicle bearing that index
number was owned by the manager of a plant-hire company,
Eric Jones, who lived at Wrexham in Denbighshire, more than
a hundred miles away. He was a married man, aged forty-five,
and was suspected by Wrexham police of being an abortionist.

Now this was really interesting.

Kim Newell had grown up on a farm estate at Rhosmadoc,
near Ruabon – about five miles from Wrexham. During
inquiries already made about her in that area, the name of
Eric Jones had been mentioned as a man with whom she had
associated before she left Wales at the age of eighteen.

Arthur Wooldridge and Peter Hill went to Wrexham to see
Jones. At first he said he had never been to Reading in his
life and did not even know where it was, though when pressed
he admitted that on 2 March he had driven to London to
negotiate some business regarding a contract in South Africa.
At a second interview, when it was clear that we had acquired
more information, Jones admitted visiting Reading on 2 March
and spending a short time with Kim Newell.

He said this came about because on his way home from
London he had lost his way in heavy traffic and found himself
travelling towards Reading instead of Birmingham. He
decided to go to Reading and telephone Newell, hoping she
would put him on the right road. He knew where she lived in
Reading because earlier that year she had telephoned him at
Wrexham and asked if he could get her anything to terminate
her pregnancy. When he saw her at Reading, she asked if he
had managed "to get the stuff". He told her he had not.

"I asked her if she could put me on the Birmingham road
and she said I had to go through Oxford," Jones contineud.
"We drove around Reading and she showed me the road to
Oxford. I dropped her off outside her house and I have not
seen or heard from her since. . . . I can't tell you for certain
where I was at ten o'clock that night, but I was well out of
Reading and on my way back to Wrexham . . . certainly on
the Birmingham side of Oxford at that time."

His Cortina yielded no clues to show that it was the mystery

Ford, and neither Franklin nor Pinfield nor Angus MacDonald could give us any description of the driver.

I was sure Jones was lying. His account of events read like a children's fairy story, but how could we disprove it? I decided to leave him with a dose of insomnia in the hope that it would eventually contribute to his cracking-up when we were equipped to go in heavy with some tough interrogation.

It was time for another wee chat with the fascinating Miss Newell. She confirmed Jones's story of his trip to London and arrival in Reading, and she did more. She admitted that she had appealed to Jones to perform an abortion on her because he had done so before, when he had made her pregnant some six years earlier. She referred to a number of telephone calls between herself and Jones on the subject of a possible abortion.

Then I got an accurate insight into her true nature. She told me that, despite her pregnancy, she had no intention of marrying Raymond Cook, even if it ever became possible. He was prepared to support her until his child was born and that was enough for her. She added, "I told him that if he did not support me, I would tell his wife about my pregnancy." I had her first admission of blackmail. When it was added to the motives of sex and greed already established, the picture became formidable.

At first I had visualized Newell as a key witness against Cook, but my views were rapidly changing. Having already formed the opinion that Cook must have had one or more accomplices, I saw Newell emerging as one of them. Was Jones another? Were those telephone calls more concerned with a plan to murder Mrs Cook than they were with abortion?

When almost one's entire adult life has revolved around crime and criminals, one develops a peculiar sixth sense. In any investigation one gets a feeling of what's right and what's wrong with the picture of a crime and the criminals involved.

There have been many occasions when I have experienced this strange feeling. A decision has to be made. Sometimes, despite circumstantial evidence, one decides that a principal suspect is innocent and then work has to start all over again. In other situations – and these are far more frustrating – an investigation has to be concluded at a point when one is positive that others are guilty but there is insufficient evidence upon which a prosecution can be based.

On Saturday, 15 April 1967, I decided that I simply must have some clean shirts. That is no doubt rather a let-down for readers of fiction whose favourite detective bounds through the pages being beaten up, jumping in and out of bed with delectable popsies, and discovering a corpse a chapter, but it was a mundane fact. Sergeant Hill and I had averaged an eighteen-hour working day from the time we arrived in Reading, so we decided to return to our London homes to catch up on some sleep and collect fresh clothing.

Newell and Jones had a lot more questions to answer, and I resolved that on the Monday I would go to Wrexham with Arthur Wooldridge and subject Jones to some hard investigation.

At 5 p.m. on Saturday, however, Wooldridge phoned me at home. "I've something to tell you – and it's dynamite!" he said. And it was. In fact, it blew the case wide open.

Kim Newell's married sister, Janette Adams, and her husband Kenneth, who lived at Thatcham, Berkshire, had walked into Newbury Police Station and said they had information regarding Mrs Cook's murder. For nearly a month this unhappy couple had been fighting a battle between loyalty to a member of the family and the dictates of conscience. Finally they had decided they could keep silent no longer, and they told the whole story.

Kim Newell, who had been under terrific strain from crime reporters constantly calling at her home, interviews with the police, and the knowledge that Cook was in prison, had reached the point where she had to confide in someone. Naturally enough, she chose her sister.

She told Mrs Adams that she and Cook had arranged with Jones that he should come to Reading and "kidnap" Mrs Cook and keep her out of their way. But Jones had completely lost his head, gone quite berserk and battered the poor woman about the head with his car-jack.

I told Wooldridge I would be with him as soon as possible, but before I left home I received another call from him – this time to say that Newell had arrived at Newbury Police Station and was most upset and angry at the "audacity" of the police in interviewing her sister. I told Wooldridge, "Never mind her tantrums. Take her to Reading Police Station and keep her there until I arrive."

I saw Kim Newell soon after I got back to Reading late that night, but she refused to tell me anything. Early the next morning she asked to see Wooldridge, saying quite frankly that she was afraid of me because she had lied to me in previous interviews. She made a long statement to Wooldridge in which she told a quite fantastic story.

She said that she and Cook had met Jones in Chester some time before Christmas 1966, when they discussed her pregnancy and told Jones that Cook could not marry her because he already had a wife. Jones began bragging and telling ludicrous stories of how he had "lost" the wives of a number of men by pushing them in their cars down bottomless mineshafts. He had been well paid for these services. He also spoke of taking women away, drugging them and keeping them for six months so that their husbands could file divorce petitions on the grounds of desertion.

According to Newell, the arrangement for 2 March was for Jones to waylay the Cooks and kidnap Mrs Cook. She (Newell) had been persuaded to show Jones the rendezvous-point earlier that evening. The first she knew of Mrs Cook's death was when she read about it in a newspaper on the following day. Cook told her that Jones had killed Mrs Cook with the car-jack and that when Cook had tried to protect his wife, Jones had threatened to kill Cook, Kim and the Cook children.

All the time she was making her statement – in a remarkably cool and collected manner – Kim Newell was taking care to lay the blame on Jones and to protect Cook. None of it rang true to me, and I was sure that this whole story of drugging, kidnapping and divorce was arrant nonsense and simply a ruse to hide the real truth, that the three of them were planning to "remove" June Cook.

At an earlier stage in the inquiry we had interviewed a girlfriend and neighbour of Newell's called Susan Heslop, but she told us nothing of any consequence. I felt at the time that Mrs Heslop was hiding something, so after Newell had made her statement I had this young woman brought to Reading Police Station for further questioning.

This time she told us a most revealing story about a terrifying afternoon she had spent with Kim Newell and three men from

Wrexham, explaining that she had kept quiet till then because she did not want her husband, Michael, to know about her involvement and was frightened of having to go to court and answer a lot of questions.

"I've been worried about it ever since, particularly when you came and questioned me," she said, "but I was just petrified." We soon found out why.

Some time early in 1967, Kim Newell asked Susan Heslop if she would go with her to meet someone at Reading railway station. In the refreshment room the two girls met three men who were unknown to Mrs Heslop. They were, in fact, Eric Jones, his brother-in-law Benjamin Jones, and his son Trevor. After they had all had cups of tea, one of the men said, "Well, let's get going, then. You can show us the place."

They got into a car, with Kim sitting next to the driver to give directions. As they drove into the countryside, there was some general talk between Kim and the three men about "getting rid of" Mrs Cook. One of the men asked, "What about Sue – can she be trusted?" and Kim replied, "Oh yes, she's all right." Another of the men said, "So Ray's going to get her drunk, then," and Kim replied, "Yes, that's right."

Newell told Mrs Heslop that Cook was going to have a quarrel with his wife in a pub because he knew that she would then leave him and drive home by herself.

"When we got to this pub, the three fellows got out and Kim stayed in the car," continued Mrs Heslop. "I was petrified out of my life. Who wouldn't be? I had heard what they had all been saying and it was obvious to me that they were planning to kill Mrs Cook. I was angry and frightened at the same time and I said to Kim, 'This is bloody ridiculous, getting me mixed up in this.' The men then got back into the car and we drove to a little bridge. Again the three men got out and Kim stayed in the car with me. One of the men said to the others, 'We'll make it look like an accident.' I told Kim that they would never make it look like an accident and that the police were too clever and would find out, but she said, 'Oh, they'll never find out.' On the way back to Reading they were talking about getting rid of Mrs Cook and one of them said, 'It's all right. We've got it all worked out now. She's got to be drunk, drive off herself, come over the bridge and into the river.' I can't remember just what Kim said, but the conversation was general and it was all about getting rid of Mrs Cook. . . . I knew they were planning to murder her."

When they arrived back in Reading, one of the men asked Newell, "Are you sure you want this done?" Newell replied that she did. Mrs Heslop, although very nervous, pleaded, "Don't do it – for goodness sake, don't do it." This seemed to create some uncertainty and Newell was asked again if she was sure she wanted it done. She hesitated momentarily before replying, "Yes, do it."

After the men had left, Mrs Heslop had told Newell that she felt that she ought to go to the police. Kim got very cross and said, "Don't be so stupid. If you don't say anything, they'll never find out." Later that evening Kim visited Sue Heslop in her flat and told her, "It's all right. You can put your mind at rest. They aren't going to do it."

Mrs Heslop told us that she and Newell remained on friendly terms. When Kim told her, some weeks later, that Mrs Cook had died in a car accident, Mrs Heslop at first believed this to be the truth. Later, however, she felt that Kim was lying.

All my suspicions of Jones had been confirmed, and, with Wooldridge and Sergeant Hill, I headed for Wrexham. This time, Jones was far more talkative.

I was curious to know how Jones had got himself involved in this fantastic affair. I found that he, like Cook, had been blackmailed by Newell, who had told him that either he organized the killing of her lover's wife or she would go to Jones's wife and tell her that he had made her (Newell) pregnant when she was sixteen and had performed abortions on her then and on several subsequent occasions. She also threatened to tell Mrs Jones that Jones had performed abortions on other girls.

It was clear that Jones had been subjected to considerable pressure. He was happily married to his second wife and felt he had little option but to do what Newell wanted, but by the time I saw him on that day in April 1967, he seemed almost keener to face a jail sentence than to go on living under Newell's blackmail threats.

Gradually, the whole horrific story emerged of four plans to kill June Cook so that her husband could inherit her estate and enjoy it with Kim Newell.

In late November or early December 1966, Newell had contacted Jones. Accompanied by Cook, whom she introduced as her new boy-friend, she met Jones in a Chinese restaurant in Chester. Jones asked if she had arranged the meeting because she wanted another abortion. She replied, "No, it's something bigger than that." Newell said she wanted Jones to smash a Mini, but at that time made no mention of anyone being in the car. She said that Cook's wife owned the Mini, but if it was smashed beyond repair, Cook could obtain the insurance money for himself and he and Newell could go away together. Jones was offered £300. He thought it would be easy to smash a Mini and told them to let him know what arrangements were made.

Later, in a telephone call, Newell said she would see that Jones got a thousand pounds, and added, "We want to get rid of Mrs Cook."

Fearful of exposure, Jones agreed to think about the idea. In another telephone call Kim Newell told him that she would soon visit Wrexham as she knew of a place where the Mini, with Mrs Cook inside, could be sunk in the River Dee. The trio met and Newell put a hundred pounds on a shelf in Jones's car, saying, "Now you can afford to take time off to run around and find somewhere." She added that Cook and his wife would travel to North Wales for the New Year and suggested that Jones should meet them.

On 30 December 1966 he received another call from Newell, this time speaking from her family home in Rhosmadoc. She said that Cook was travelling with his wife to North Wales and would meet Jones that evening at the Goat public house near Llangollen, Denbighshire – which is on the banks of the River Dee.

She gave Jones the number of the Mini. While Jones was looking at it in the car park, Cook came out of the hotel and said, "You can't do anything. The will hasn't been changed." This was the first time Jones had heard anything about a will. Mrs Cook suddenly walked out of the hotel and the conversation was quickly turned to lighter matters. Cook, pretending they were strangers, began asking Jones about the best hotels in the area. Jones named one, and later, while he was drinking there with friends, the Cooks arrived.

Kim Newell telephoned again a few days later from Reading and confirmed that if Mrs Cook was murdered at that time,

Cook would not benefit from the will, because it stood in favour of the Cooks' sons.

She said she would find a murder-spot in Berkshire and would phone again. In subsequent calls, she repeatedly asked about an abortion. At the first meeting between Jones, Cook and Newell, the girl said her reason for contacting Jones was not because she wanted an abortion – but some time after Christmas 1966, she told Jones she was pregnant and asked him to help her get rid of the unborn child.

"She said she and Ray would get married when and if he got a divorce," said Jones. "To be honest I thought it was funny, her trying to settle down, because I didn't think she was the type."

Newell kept telephoning Jones and pestering him about an abortion. Jones told her he had not been able to "get the stuff". She was furious and threatened to tell Mrs Jones. On several occasions Jones's wife answered the telephone when Newell called, and each time Newell rang off without speaking. This made Mrs Jones suspicious, and she accused her husband of having an affair with another woman. Jones pleaded with Newell to stop telephoning, but the girl only laughed and said, "I haven't spoken to her, have I?" She continued to telephone frequently, and on one occasion threatened to expose Jones to the police as well as to his wife. She said she had been talking to a policeman with whom she was acquainted and he had told her that eight years' jail was the sentence for illegal abortion.

Jones, getting desperate by this time because his wife was threatening to leave him, begged Newell to stop the phone calls.

"Well, it's not as bad as eight years, is it?" laughed Kim.

About the end of January 1967, Jones met Newell and Cook in the buffet at Shrewsbury Station. At first they talked about the proposed abortion, but then Newell said she had found a place near Reading where she thought the Mini could be run into the river. This was on the River Blackwater, near a public house at Swallowfield, a village six miles from Reading.

This time the plan was for Cook to take his wife to the public house and get her drunk. She would then be put into the car and Jones would drive it away and jump clear before it ran into the river. Cook was to tell the people in the pub that his wife had driven off without him and would no doubt return to pick him up. This would give Jones time to get to his own car and drive away.

Jones and the girl went to Reading to take a look at the proposed locale for this "accident", but Jones decided that the water was too shallow.

The telephone calls to Jones's house were resumed, and eventually Newell said she had found another place where the water was deeper. Under pressure, Jones made another trip to Reading. This was the occasion on which he was accompanied by his son and brother-in-law and met Newell and Sue Heslop at Reading railway station.

They went to view the new site – the Black Bridge, Sandford, over the River Loddon, a couple of miles outside Reading. The Mini, with Mrs Cook inside, was to be pushed off a concrete ramp. Cook was going to take his wife to the Falcon public house near the bridge, where he would stage a quarrel and walk out on her. When she started to drive home alone, Jones would stop her, get into the car and run it into the river.

Jones objected to this plan because he could not swim and was likely to drown himself as well as Mrs Cook, and he also made the excuse that it was not safe because Mrs Heslop had overheard some of their conversation. Kim Newell was furious, saying "It's got to happen tonight. Everything's fixed. Ray's taking his wife out this evening." She told Jones, however, that if he did not intend to carry out the plan he should telephone Cook and say that "the cricket match" was off – Cook shared a party-line with his mother-in-law, and Newell was scared that Mrs Garrett might be listening. Jones phoned Cook, used this code-message and then drove back to Wrexham. I checked the proposed murder-scene. The drop from the edge of the ramp to the water was five feet and the depth was six feet. At the time the "accident" was to have occurred, the water would have been deep enough to conceal the Mini from anyone passing along the road.

Soon after this, Cook telephoned Jones, spoke of "looking at another place" and asked for a definite date. Jones made excuses and said he was very busy. Within days Newell was back on the line, complaining angrily because no date had been fixed and making more threats of exposure. She told

Jones that Cook was again living with his wife, who had
restored the will to his favour, and stressed the need for haste
in carrying out their plans.

Eventually, Eric Jones agreed to visit Reading on 2 March
1967. He drove to Sidmouth Street to pick up Newell, who
had a piece of paper with a map drawn on it. They went to
Rumerhedge Wood, where she outlined the murder plot,
telling Jones where he was to park and indicating where Cook
would stop the Mini. It was on their return-journey to Reading
– Newell insisted she be driven back – that the pair were seen
by Angus MacDonald.

Cook was to take his wife to dinner at the George Hotel,
Pangbourne. They would then drive through the wood – a
considerable detour – on the pretext that it "would make a
change". Then Jones was to flag him down, using the excuse
that his blue Ford Cortina had a puncture.

"If Ray isn't there on time, I'm going home because I
promised to be back by midnight and there'll be an awful lot
of trouble otherwise," Jones said to Kim Newell.

"If you leave here tonight without doing it, you'll get into
a lot more bloody trouble," she retorted. "I'll be on the phone
to the police by ten o'clock in the morning and you'll get eight
years for abortion."

I finally obtained the true story of what happened that night
from Jones. He was a man consumed with terror. He was
terrified of Kim Newell, terrified of the law.

The sleepless nights he had suffered following the first interview with Wooldridge had taken their toll – as I'd anticipated.
He cracked.

He told me that Newell had pointed out a tree in
Rumerhedge Wood and said, "That's the one. You have
nothing to worry about. All you have to do is pick the Mini
up where I showed you, run it into the tree and help make it
look like an accident. Ray will see to her. After that, you'll
have to punch him on the chin and knock him out."

She assured Jones that Mrs Cook would be drunk, but would
not tell him how she was to be killed. Jones repeatedly asked
how it was to be done, but all Newell would say was, "He'll
see to her . . . he's been a medical student."

Jones drove Newell back to Reading and immediately

returned to the scene selected for Mrs Cook's murder. The appointed time was 9.30 p.m.

"I didn't have a watch on me and didn't know how long I would have to wait, but I knew it was going to be a long time," Jones said. "As I waited there, I had a good think to myself. I didn't think Cook would have the guts to kill his wife, and if he wanted me to do it I would sidestep it. There was no means of doing it, so far as I was aware. I wanted to go home, but I daren't. I cried. It may sound stupid, but it's true. Newell had me, but I hoped that something would crop up so that I could get out of it."

After a while, Jones left the wood and drove to the Fox public house at Cane End for a drink, staying only for about ten minutes. This part of Jones's account of his movements tied up one or two loose ends that had been bothering me. When the first inquiries about the "accident" were being made, we were told of the blue Cortina by the witnesses Pinfield and Franklin, who were on the scene at ten o'clock. We also took a statement from a local farmer, who confirmed that a blue Cortina was parked on the road through the wood at about 9.20 p.m. What puzzled me at the time, but helped to prove the truth of Jones's statement, was that another driver passing that way, a Mr Douglas Borton, was emphatic that there was no vehicle of any kind parked on the road when he drove through at about 9.30. It is clear that Borton drove through the wood during Jones's visit to the Fox.

Hesitantly, Jones spoke of the actual killing.

"I was frightened," he said. "I hoped something would happen to enable me to sidestep it. My mouth was dry and I was shivering and shuddering. I got out of the car. I had a pair of rubber gloves in the boot and I put them on and went round the Cortina, cleaning the windscreen, lamps and radiator. I couldn't sit still. I had to do something. I walked down to the tree, for no reason really other than to pass the time.

"Two cars passed, one right behind the other. I left the boot open and it was still open when the Mini came along with Cook driving. He went past a few yards and stopped. He got out and I waited for him to walk up to me. I expected him to take Mrs Cook out of the Mini. I thought that would be the first move. I spoke first. I said, 'You can't do nothing. Cars are running up and down like hell.' He just mumbled something at first, then he said, 'Let's get on with it.'

"I said I'd go over to Mrs Cook as he told me she was in the car. I went to the passenger door and put my hand on the handle. I went to open the door. I expected to find her awful drunk. They had said she would be drunk and I expected I would have to help her out or even lift her out of the car. . . . I said again, 'You can't do nothing. She doesn't know anything about it.' That doesn't make sense, but my reason for saying it was because she was not as drunk as I had expected.

"Cook said, 'Come along,' and nudged me on the elbow. I told Cook that I couldn't run the car into the tree without some excuse to get inside. We walked to the driver's door and he opened it and leaned through. He said to Mrs Cook, 'He's got a flat tyre. He wants a foot-pump. Do you mind if we give him a lift to town?' I didn't hear her say anything. Cook pulled the driver's seat forward to allow me to get into the back seat. I don't know why I got into the back, but it looked as though he meant me to get in there. . . . Cook didn't get in, but walked away from the car.

"After that everything happened very quickly. Mrs Cook leaned across the driver's seat and started shouting, 'Ray!' She put her hand up in front of me. I hadn't moved or said anything. . . . She continued to shout, 'Ray!' as if in a panic. I got frightened myself and pushed the seat forward to get out of the car, as it was my being in the car that frightened her. She was holding the seat so I couldn't get out. It looked as if she wanted her husband back. I took hold of her. . . . I punched her on the jaw with my right hand. I don't know how hard I hit her.

"I tried again to get out by pushing the seat. I got partly out but couldn't get right out as she got hold of my jacket and trousers with both hands. . . . I was going out backwards and I got one foot on the ground. This foot slipped and I hit my shin on the door sill. . . . She kept shouting for Ray. Her head was down and it didn't seem so loud. I was in a panic now. I was punching like hell. In my panic it flashed through my mind that Cook would strike me from the back. He appeared on the right between the door and me.

"I had my left hand down, trying to push her away. . . . I felt Cook's arm come down on my forearm and he said, 'Here.'

The murder-weapon

I turned round and the jack was by my face. He was holding it in his hand. At that time I had no idea what it was. I snatched it out of his hand. In that split second I thought he might hit me with it. . . . I brought it down on Mrs Cook's head. . . . I can only remember hitting her once but it might have been more. I wanted to get away from the screaming woman and Cook. My only intention was to get away from it. I didn't intend to kill her at that moment.

"The next thing I remember was sitting in my car. The key wasn't in the dashboard. The sweat was running into my eyes. My mouth was bone-dry. I don't know where Cook was at this time. I don't know where the jack was either. I got out of my car to get the key from the boot-lid. Before I could remove the key, Cook shouted and came towards me. I walked back towards him. I said, 'We're in trouble now,' and he replied, 'You might as well smash it now you're here. . . .' He seemed quite cool. He walked to the other side of the Mini and I went to the driver's side.

"I thought about the worry I had had from Valerie Newell

and it didn't take any thinking about. Her last threats had made it very clear to me what she would do. . . . I knew I couldn't do anything else. I had no idea how seriously injured Mrs Cook was. I just seemed to go automatically. It seems stupid now, but I tried to take Mrs Cook out of the car.

"She was sitting in the driver's seat, leaning over the wheel. . . . When I tried to lift her sideways, I heard the blood plop on the floor. . . . I had to push her over. . . . I wanted to get in and sit on the seat, but I didn't have enough room, so I stood on the sill with my right foot on the throttle, held the inside of the roof with my left hand and steered with my right. Cook started it off and put it in gear. I steered it to the left round the bend. I intended hitting the tree, but my right hand slipped with the blood on the rim of the steering wheel and came down hard on the spoke and this caused the car to turn sharp right. It hit the tree but I almost missed it."

Jones lifted Mrs Cook out of the car and scraped some leaves together to lay her head on. Cook reappeared and put something on the ground beside Jones, saying, "If she's gone we'll be all right." Jones said that Mrs Cook was still breathing.

Slowly, Jones went on: "I think it was then that I felt my gloves were slipping and realized it was with blood. I started thinking of the worry I had had keeping out of it and realized what I had done. I was frightened and in despair. I felt I was finished. I knew I had done it. I was mad at Newell then, more than mad, and I picked up this thing that Cook had put down. It was the jack. I turned to my right and hit her [Mrs Cook] on the head. If I had had a gun I would have shot myself."

At that moment Franklin and Pinfield rounded the bend. As Jones saw the lights of their car approaching, he hit Mrs Cook again. "I knew nothing could be done to help," he said.

Just before these witnesses arrived, Cook said to Jones, "You'd better knock me out." Jones retorted, "You can knock your fucking self out if it's going to do you any good." He did not hit Cook.

Jones picked up the jack and took it back to his own car after Franklin had spoken to him. He drove all the way to Wrexham without stopping. The following morning, he threw the jack into a yachting pool known as Gresford Flash, three

Raymond Cook, flanked by detectives, in a police-car after his arrest

miles from Wrexham. It was later recovered by the Liverpool City Police Underwater Search Unit.

Right up to her arrest, Kim Newell was still trying to manipulate her men. Two days before Jones was arrested, she wrote to him:

> Dear Eric,
>   Sorry to have got you into all this trouble. Don't worry. Don't tell the police any more than you have done. I have seen Ray and he won't bend. He is sticking to his statement that she was dazzled on the corner. We will not bring you into it.
>
>   Love, Val.

When the murderous trio stood in the dock before Mr Justice Stable at Oxfordshire Assizes in June 1967, Jones and Cook were jointly charged with the murder of Mrs Cook. Valerie Newell was accused of being an accessory before the fact "in that she counselled, procured and hired" the two men to commit the murder.

All three pleaded Not Guilty at first, but Jones later changed his plea to Guilty and was called as a witness for the prosecution. In court he stuck to the story he had told me. Under cross-examination by Mr William Howard, counsel for Valerie Newell, he admitted that he first met the girl in a school playground when he was thirty-seven and she was sixteen, that she became pregnant as a result of their association, and that he performed an abortion on her.

Valerie Newell, who was in an advanced state of pregnancy by the time she stood trial, pleaded Not Guilty. She said she thought Jones was going to kidnap Mrs Cook and did not know that she was to be harmed in any way.

She was questioned by Mr Brian Gibbens, prosecuting, about her association with Raymond Cook.

"The whole aspect was that you had to have money in order to keep on living with him and you could not get money without the removal of Mrs Cook?" asked Mr Gibbens.

"That is not true," replied Newell. "I did not know about his financial affairs."

"Would you not agree that throughout the time you have known him, Mr Cook was a sort of silent lumpkin who did as you bid him?"

"No, no, not throughout the time."

When Newell said she thought Cook was fond of his wife, Mr Gibbens asked her: "Notwithstanding that he was living with you and getting you pregnant, was going to have his wife abducted, get a divorce and marry you?"

"We did not talk about marriage," answered Newell.

At this point Mr Justice Stable leaned forward, thumped the bench with his fist and asked her, "Well, what *did* you want?"

"I didn't mind if he went back to his wife or not."

Raymond Cook cut a poor figure in the witness-box. Pleading Not Guilty to the murder of his wife, he said he was given to understand that Jones might be able to arrange something "on the lines of a divorce". When they met at the appointed place on the night of 2 March, he thought Jones was going to drug his wife with chloroform. He agreed that he did not make any serious attempt to stop Jones attacking his wife with the jack, adding, "I have never used violence against anybody."

When Mr Gibbens, holding the jack in his hand, asked,

"Here was a man slaughtering your wife – and because you never used violence to any man before, you didn't think of trying to save your wife?" Cook made no reply.

Mr Gibbens asked him why he could not continue living with Miss Newell without the removal of his wife. Cook replied, "My wife's health was not good."

Summing up for the Crown, Mr Gibbens also summed up my own feelings when he said that it was Valerie Newell who provided the motive and means while she kept safe and sound behind the scenes.

"There have been women in history who have done that," he said. "Lady Macbeth got her husband to commit murder while she remained aside. Like Lady Macbeth, this woman was urging her lover to 'screw his courage to the sticking place'. He was in her grip. Cook thought it was for marriage and love. She thought of nothing except money. . . . In the witness box she presented herself to you with a wide-eyed innocence, but does she finish up such an innocent maiden as at first she seemed? You may think you have seen a very clever, very ruthless and dangerous woman. . . . What sort of morality does this woman have? What sort of truth do you think she worships? She was not interested in marriage or Cook. She was out for money."

Raymond Cook, Eric Jones and Valerie Newell were all sentenced to life imprisonment. Mr Justice Stable commended the police team which investigated the murder, making particular reference to PC Sherlock.

Seven weeks after she was sentenced, Valerie Newell became the mother of a 6lb son. Five months later, the Court of Appeal refused both Newell and Cook leave to appeal.

Looking for Baby-Face

Thomas M. McDade

THERE IS a faded photograph on my wall that goes back more than half a century. It is a snapshot of me standing beside a black Ford coupé, and was taken by my partner Bill Ryan in early November 1934 on the Chicago North Drive. I had moved to Chicago from Washington, DC, two months before, having just completed the FBI training course for recruits, and I still felt very much like the new boy at school. A block away from where the photo was taken, Ryan and I had an apartment where we maintained a telephone-tap on the sister of a dangerous fugitive. The tap did not prove very productive, but it accounted for our being there on 27 November and for what followed.

That day, Ryan, a veteran of several years in the Chicago office, left the apartment to call Inspector Sam Cowley, who was our boss in Chicago. When he returned, he told me that it was believed that Baby-Face Nelson (real name Lester Gillis) had been seen at Lake Geneva, Wisconsin, and that we were to join other agents in that area.

At that time Nelson was the most wanted man in the country. He was the last major member of the Dillinger gang who had not been killed or captured. He had escaped an FBI trap at Little Bohemia, Wisconsin, in April, killing one of the agents and wounding a policeman. A vicious psychopath, his hair-trigger temper made his own companions so leery of him that they often left him to divide the loot of their bank heists rather than risk unpleasantness. Dillinger had died in July; Nelson had simply vanished.

As we drove towards Lake Geneva on the Northwest Highway, Ryan filled me in on the background of the search for Nelson. Among the girls left behind at Little Bohemia, there was one who had agreed to help the agents. In describing her travels with the gang, she had mentioned visiting a house at Lake Geneva where Nelson was known and made welcome. To locate this house, she had driven around the area with an agent until she finally recognized it. The owner, a man named Cobe, had admitted that Nelson had stayed there in the past and that he was sure he would return sooner or later. He had agreed to let two FBI men live in the house with him and his wife Ruth, and Agents Charlie Winstead and Jimmy Metcalfe had moved in.

That very morning, Winstead had been in an upstairs bedroom cleaning a rifle while overlooking the driveway when a maroon sedan drove in and stopped a short distance from the house. He had shouted to Metcalfe, who was downstairs, and Metcalfe, looking out of the window at the car, had said, "That's Ruth." He had previously helped Mrs Cobe with her bundles, and now he stepped on to the porch in his shirt-sleeves, intending to offer further assistance. But the minute he got outside, he realized that he had misidentified the car. The driver, a man, shouted to him, asking for Cobe. Metcalfe said he was in town and would be back soon. While this exchange was going on, Metcalfe was trying to identify the driver and passengers – a woman in the front passenger-seat, a man in the back. The car drove off. Stepping back into the house, Metcalfe shouted to Winstead that he thought the

WANTED

LESTER M. GILLIS,

aliases GEORGE NELSON, "BABY FACE" NELSON, ALEX GILLIS, LESTER GILES, "BIG GEORGE" NELSON, "JIMMIE", "JIMMY" WILLIAMS.

On June 23, 1934, HOMER S. CUMMINGS, Attorney General of the United States, under the authority vested in him by an Act of Congress approved June 6, 1934, offered a reward of

$5,000.00

for the capture of Lester M. Gillis or a reward of

$2,500.00

for information leading to the arrest of Lester M. Gillis.

DESCRIPTION

Age, 25 years; Height, 5 feet 4-3/4 inches; Weight, 133 pounds; Build, medium; Eyes, yellow and gray slate; Hair, light chestnut; Complexion, light; Occupation, oiler.

All claims to any of the aforesaid rewards and all questions and disputes that may arise as among claimants to the foregoing rewards shall be passed upon by the Attorney General and his decisions shall be final and conclusive. The right is reserved to divide and allocate portions of any of said rewards as between several claimants. No part of the aforesaid rewards shall be paid to any official or employee of the Department of Justice.

If you are in possession of any information concerning the whereabouts of Lester M. Gillis, communicate immediately by telephone or telegraph collect to the nearest office of the Division of Investigation, United States Department of Justice, the local offices of which are set forth on the reverse side of this notice.

The apprehension of Lester M. Gillis is sought in connection with the murder of Special Agent W. C. Baum of the Division of Investigation near Rhinelander, Wisconsin on April 23, 1934.

JOHN EDGAR HOOVER, DIRECTOR,
DIVISION OF INVESTIGATION,
UNITED STATES DEPARTMENT OF JUSTICE,
WASHINGTON, D. C.

June 20, 1934

driver was Nelson. The Illinois plate-number – 639-578 – was of a current licence.

Winstead had immediately telephoned Sam Cowley in Chicago, and it was on the basis of that call that we were now on our way to Lake Geneva. I suggested to Ryan that he write the number out, and we pinned the note over the windshield so that I could see it as I drove and check on-coming cars. Cowley had asked Ryan what weapons we had, and had been told that we only had handguns. Mine was a .38 calibre revolver, Ryan's a "super" .38 automatic pistol.

The road north to Lake Geneva, forty miles from Chicago, passes through Fox River Grove. Ryan recalled that there was a bar there which the gangs frequented. As we drove through Fox River Grove, we paused to look over the place, but there were no cars parked nearby and it appeared to be closed. We continued along the highway, watching all the cars coming towards us. Suddenly, as a car went past us, I shouted to Ryan:

"*Five seven eight.*"

"There were two men and a woman in the car," Ryan said. I had slowed down, uncertain what to do.

Ryan pointed ahead. "Go down the road to where that turn is and make your turn there."

I continued down the road about two hundred yards, then turned and headed back the way we had come. As I did so, Ryan, who had been watching through the rear window, said, "They've turned round. They're coming back." We passed each other again, but I was so concentrated on the licence number that I never saw the people in the car. Simultaneously we shouted the plate number: "639-578". Ryan turned to continue watching them and almost immediately announced, "They've turned again. They're right behind us".

I looked in the rear-view mirror and saw the car a short way back. I was very uneasy about our position.

"I think we ought to stay ahead of them," I said.

"No, no," said Ryan, "let them catch up to us so we can get a good look at them." I had reservations about that, but Ryan was the old-timer and I continued down the highway at about forty miles an hour. Ryan had taken out his pistol, assured himself that there was a cartridge in the chamber, and held it between his knees. I kept my eyes ahead, expecting the other car to pass us.

Suddenly there was a car-horn blowing next to me and I turned to look, waiting for the car to pass. Instead, almost alongside us, I saw the driver shouting and waving his arm to us to pull over. There was a woman in the seat next to him, and behind was a man cradling an automatic rifle aimed in our direction. Ryan bent down to look across me and immediately sat up.

"We've got to get out of here," was all he said. The words were barely out of him than I had jammed the pedal to the floor. We shot down the road. Almost immediately we heard shots. Acutely conscious that too much of my six foot four inches showed in the back window, I slid down in the seat as much as I could. I could no longer see through the rearview mirror. The sound of shots continued and I had a clear impression that they were hitting the car. I remember once looking at the speedometer and reading seventy-five m.p.h.

The Northwest Highway was only a two-lane road and I was thinking about what I would do if I could not pass a car in front of me. Ryan, meanwhile, started to return the fire, shooting through our back window. Bits of glass and empty shells were ejected in my direction.

"Where are they? Where are they?" I shouted.

"They're right behind us. Step on it."

He turned and began reloading the clip of his automatic.

Taking a quick look over his shoulder, he announced, "They've fallen back." As he said this, I slid up to look myself and saw them a couple of hundred yards behind. Looking ahead, I saw a truck. I started to pass it. Coming towards me in the opposite lane was another car. Having to choose between the hazard behind me and the danger of passing, I opted for the latter and shot through a narrowing space. We continued south at high speed.

"We'll be coming to Barrington soon. It's a sharp turn right. You'll have to slow down." Ryan told me, still looking back.

I could see the turn approaching. I began slowing down, but as we started to turn, the scream of the tyres told me were going much too fast. There was a field on the left, so I let the car run off the road into it. I managed to stop well back in a meadow. Ryan jumped out one side and I the other. We looked for our pursuers, but they were nowhere to be seen.

After a short spell of waiting, we drove into Barrington and Ryan went to a phone to report to the office. He was back in a short while with the instructions that we were to continue to Chicago and check in by phone in thirty minutes.

While Ryan was phoning, I had examined the car. I was

puzzled to find no sign of the bullets which I thought had hit it. I didn't solve that mystery until a few days later. We drove slowly back to Chicago. I felt drained and exhausted. Once more we stopped to call the office. When Ryan left the phone booth, his face was ashen and he could hardly speak.

"They killed Hollis," he said. "Cowley has been shot, and Nelson got away in the Bureau car." I tried to take in what he was saying. According to the office agents, Cowley and Hollis had been driving to Lake Geneva on the road behind us. They had encountered Nelson's car and a gun-battle had ensued. The details were still vague. We started once more on our return – very uneasy about the sight of the bullet-holes which Ryan's gun had made in our rear window. All the roads would now be watched by the police, and we didn't want to be mistaken for the Bureau car they were hunting. Eventually we slipped into the city and dropped the car at the Bureau garage.

Bob Hicks, one of the agents, greeted me in the office: "My God, you're white as a sheet." I wasn't up to explaining but I wanted to know about Cowley and Hollis.

They had been driving on the road behind us and must have seen Nelson pursuing us. On the near side of Barrington, Nelson had suddenly turned off the road and jumped out of his car. Hollis drove about a hundred yards down the road before stopping. He stood behind his Hudson sedan with a shot-gun; Cowley ran into a ditch by the side of the road with a machine-gun. Nelson walked straight down the road with a rifle. Both agents fired at Nelson as he walked towards them, seemingly without being hit. When Hollis had emptied the shot-gun, he started to run from behind the car to a field across the road, but he never made it. He was hit in the head as he ran and was killed instantly. Cowley was hit in the stomach. Nelson got into the Hudson and backed it up to where his own car was standing; he and the two passengers rapidly moved their weapons and luggage to the Bureau car, and he drove off. Word had just come from the hospital that Cowley had died.

I have a vague recollection of going out that night with a party of agents searching buildings in the city. It was very late when I staggered to my room on the near North Side. I had trouble getting to sleep.

It was about noon before I got to the office, which was crowded with agents brought in from the surrounding area. I was depressed by the thought of the two dead men – by the thought that Nelson was still on the loose.

I was told that I could put the latter thought out of my mind.

Early that morning, Nelson's naked body had been found beside a road north of Chicago. He had bled to death from a bullet wound through the stomach. One of Cowley's shots had taken effect. Nor had Hollis missed. Eight slugs from his shotgun had entered Nelson's legs at the front and exited at the back. Despite those wounds, Nelson had carried on walking.

The man who had been with Nelson was identified as John Paul Chase, a minor bootlegger from California. He had disappeared. The woman in the car proved to be Helen Gillis, Nelson's wife; she surrendered a few days later.

Bit by bit, more of the picture emerged about our fight. Examination of Nelson's abandoned car revealed that one of Ryan's bullets had smashed the radiator, causing the engine to lose speed. It accounted for our getting away.

I was still puzzled by the fact that, though I had had the sensation that bullets were hitting our car, there was no sign of such damage. It now came out that Chase had been shooting through the windshield with a Browning automatic rifle. Ordinarily the bullets would have torn through our car, but the shells he was using were hollow-point bullets which flatten out when they strike anything and make a devastatingly large hole. However, as he was shooting through the windshield, the slugs flattened out and lost all their velocity and force.

In California, agents began to visit the spots where Chase was known. A couple of weeks later, in Mount Shasta, the chief of police picked up Chase on the street after being told that he was in town trying to borrow some money. He was flown back to Chicago to stand trial for the deaths of Cowley and Hollis.

I was in the office when Chase arrived, and was curious to see him. He had been put in a holding cell, and when he was finally left alone I went to the cell-door and looked in. He was in his thirties; while his face had a certain hardness in it, I recalled that all those who had spoken to him felt that if he

JOHN PAUL CHASE

had not been with someone like Nelson, he would have passed his time unnoticed in the minor rackets or bootlegging. He looked up from where he was sitting and stared at me. Then he surprised me.

"Aren't you one of the fellows who was in the other car?" he asked.

I nodded. "Yes. I was the driver."

"You had a close call," he said.

Again I nodded.

Where does the story end? Looking back on it now, it seems to have continued for years. In the Spring of 1935, Chase went to trial in Chicago; the prosecuting attorney was Dwight Green, the local district attorney, assisted by Brian McMahon, a Department of Justice attorney from Washington. Ryan and I appeared as witnesses, as did a number of people who had seen the final shootout in which the two agents were killed. Conviction was a foregone conclusion; only the penalty was in doubt. Chase was given a life sentence.

The publicity given to the trial proved beneficial to some: Green, the District Attorney, was later elected Governor of Illinois, and McMahon became a United States Senator from Connecticut and headed the Senatorial Committee on Atomic Affairs. Ryan remained an agent for a considerable time, and two of his sons followed him in that work. He died a few years ago. As for me, I stayed some years in the Bureau, had a spell in the army during the war, and finally took a position in business.

Long after the trial, I received a letter from a Catholic priest who was trying to get Chase paroled. At his request, I wrote a letter recommending that Chase be released, and I later learned that he had got out but had survived only a couple of years.

The Hit-and-Run Murderer

Bill Knox

IN THE YEAR 1895 a petrol-engined car demonstrated its ability by accomplishing the one-in-five climb of Douglas Street, Glasgow, and then attained the surprising pace of 17 mph on the level roadway. The driver, immediately cautioned and charged, was fined two shillings and sixpence for speeding.

Five years later, the Glasgow police purchased their first mobile unit. It was a bicycle. Until then, they'd only had the right to hire a horse-cab in extreme emergency. By the following year, 1901, there were no fewer than six car accidents in the city within a period of twelve months and there were widespread expressions of public horror at the new menace which threatened the citizens' safety.

But it was not until 1950 that the High Court of Justiciary in Glasgow heard its first case in which the murder weapon was alleged to be a car. When it happened, the accused was a serving Glasgow police constable, the car was stolen and was being used with false number plates, and evidence was led that he had used it frequently to give lifts to fellow officers as they went to and from duty,

At first, however, the whole affair might have been dismissed as just a rather nasty road accident caused by a hit-and-run driver.

In the very early hours of Friday, July 28 1950, a city taxi-driver was travelling along Prospecthill Road, in the Mount Florida district, when his headlights shone on the body of a woman lying on the roadway about a yard from the pavement.

He stopped, saw at a glance that the woman was dead, and called the police. At the same time a Corporation lorry drew up at the scene. The lorry driver, who was attached to a gang carrying out tram-track repairs, said that he had passed the spot about ten minutes before and had noticed a small black saloon car standing at the roadside without lights. As they had driven past, one of the work gang had said he felt sure he had seen a woman's body on the road behind the car. But, as so often happens, the driver had refused to believe him at the time.

Directed by radio, a police traffic patrol car soon joined them. One of the officers aboard was Constable William Kevin, aged forty-five, a man with fifteen years' service and a long experience of the routine of road accidents. Constable Kevin took his time over his initial inspection of the roadway.

For a start, the woman had suffered terrible injuries. He was to describe them later as "the worst injuries I've ever seen in a road accident".

Auburn hair torn and matted by blood, she wore what had been a light coat over a red dress. Probably she'd been good-looking. But now she lay on her back, legs crossed above the knee, arms by her sides, her shoes lying some distance away, her clothing heavily stained with blood and oil. Smashed fragments of her dental plate lay on the roadway.

An accident?

Constable Kevin, working by torchlight, looked again. There was no sign of the broken headlamp glass or underwing mud which he'd normally expect to find scattered around after such an impact. But there were two brake marks of tyres on the roadway, with the body lying across them. The brake marks in themselves were unusual. One was straight and the other curved and they met.

Added together, all the factors meant one thing only. He examined the brake marks again. One set had been made by a car going in a westerly direction – the mark was streaked at first, then strengthened to where it stopped at a straight edge. The second set, the curved set, gave similar indications of having been made by a car going in the opposite direction.

To the constable, it seemed certain that the woman had been lying in the road when a car had driven over her. It had stopped a little further on, perhaps with her body trapped underneath, then had reversed.

Constable Kevin called the CID. Within a very few hours the evidence found on that quiet stretch of roadway, evidence examined by police and medical experts, confirmed his judgment.

The case was murder: murder by motor car.

In that morning's newspapers, though reporters had quickly realized that something out of the ordinary was going on, the only stories which could be carried were restricted to the fact that police were searching for a car after the discovery of a woman who had apparently been knocked down and killed.

It was enough. A Glasgow woman who had agreed to look after a friend's baby for the night was already alarmed at the fact that her friend hadn't returned to collect the child. She read the story, contacted the police, and the body was identified.

The dead woman, forty-year-old Catherine McCluskey, was unmarried and had two children. She had gone out the previous evening, dressed in her best clothes and saying she had to attend to "important business".

Very soon the murder squad team had interviewed several women who had been friendly with Catherine McCluskey – and had gathered sufficient information to make this a particularly grim, particularly personal manhunt.

For Catherine McCluskey had claimed that the father of her youngest child was a policeman and that she received money from him. At least one of the women had previously seen her as the passenger in a car driven by a man in police uniform. Another said McCluskey had confided to her that the policeman's surname was Robertson and that he was a married man. To still another woman she had said that the baby's father was driving her around while she tried to find a new place to live.

Several pieces of a complex jigsaw suddenly began to fall into place.

A Glasgow Southern Division constable, No. 138D, thirty-three-year-old James Ronald Robertson, was already under an official cloud because of suspicions that he was often absent when he was supposed to be patrolling his beat in the Gorbals area. For several weeks he had been seen using a large black Austin saloon car, one which he had told colleagues he had been given on a long-term loan by a friend.

Yet until not long before, Robertson, a teetotal, non-smoking family man, brought up in a strict, religious home, had shown all the makings of a good officer. "Big Ronnie", six foot one in height, well built and good-looking, with a small dark moustache, had two commendations to his credit.

An ex-aircraft engine inspector, married with two children, his main interest was in things mechanical.

The checks began. It was quickly established that Robertson had slipped away from his beat patrol for a spell on the night of the murder.

Ironically, the police logbook at Cumberland Street signalbox, the one used by Robertson, contained an entry in his handwriting. It was a message, timed at 2.10 a.m., circulated on the morning after Catherine McCluskey's body was discovered:

> At 12.50 a.m. today a woman was knocked down and fatally injured in Prospecthill Road near Aikenhead Road. The motor car, believed to be a small blue Austin, maybe 10 h.p., was driven by a man wearing a light fawn burberry coat. The car did not stop and was last seen driving citywards in Aikenhead Road.

That night, when Robertson should have been on beat duty, he was being questioned by senior officers. The next morning, wearing civilian clothes, he appeared in court, was charged, and was remanded for inquiry. A little later, wearing uniform again for what was to be the last time, he took his place in an identity parade in which every man in the line-up was a uniformed constable. The parade was attended by several friends of the dead woman.

In the weeks that followed, while he lay in Barlinnie Prison awaiting trial, more and more evidence accumulated. The final list of witnesses in the indictment against him was one of the longest presented to the High Court for several years.

At last, on 6 November 1950, James Ronald Robertson took his place in the dock in the North Court. He was to be tried before Lord Keith and a jury of eight men and seven women – and seldom has a Scottish murder trial seen a more impressive assembly of legal ability.

The case for the Crown was presented by the Advocate Depute, Mr Harold Leslie, KC, later Lord Birsay, assisted by Mr Ian Robertson, Advocate, later Lord Robertson. Defending Robertson and then Dean of the Faculty of Advocates, Mr John Cameron, KC, later Lord Cameron, was assisted by Mr Manuel Kissen, Advocate, later Lord Kissen.

I watched while Robertson, wearing a blue lounge suit, sat with his head bowed as the indictment was read to the jury.

It charged that on 28 July he had first assaulted Catherine McCluskey by "striking her on the head with a rubber truncheon or rendering her insensibly by other means" and that he then drove a car bearing false registration plates over her and "did murder her".

There were two lesser yet related charges. The first alleged that in April that year he had broken into a motor showroom and stolen a radio and a number of car registration books. The second alleged that at the end of May he had stolen a car from a street in the city centre.

Slowly, with that particular air of restrained drama which the North Court brings forth on such occasions, the trial got under way. First came formal evidence; then, one by one, women friends of Catherine McCluskey entered the witness box to tell how she had talked about her "policeman boyfriend".

A National Assistance Board official said that when Catherine McCluskey had applied for benefit she had declined to name the father of her second child but had admitted that he was a married man and a police officer.

On the second day of the trial, the queue for admission to the public gallery began to form at 7.30 a.m., two and a half hours before the court opened. When the doors closed, every seat taken, many of the queue were still outside.

The Crown case continued. A motor trader identified the radio and fourteen registration books found in Robertson's home as ones stolen from his premises. He confirmed that one of the registration books had been altered since it was stolen. The stolen car was identified by its legal owner and by a mechanic.

The first police witnesses included Robertson's mate on Number Eight beat. In evidence, he said that Robertson had given him a lift in the car when they went on duty at 11 p.m. They parked the car in a lane and after a spell Robertson had gone off, saying he was "going to take a blonde home".

The constable explained that soon afterwards he had answered a call to help deal with a breach of the peace. Several arrests had to be made and it was twenty minutes after midnight before he returned to normal routine. There was still no sign of Robertson, and when a sergeant arrived they went together to look for the missing man.

At 1.10 a.m., as they walked along, a torch flashed and Robertson hurried to meet them. When he arrived, the collar of his shirt was wet with sweat and he had obviously been hurrying. Once the sergeant had gone, added the witness, Robertson told him that he had "had some time of it" and that the exhaust of the car had been broken.

There was more evidence which showed how, in various ways, Robertson had been secretly dodging his assigned duties.

Then the story moved on to his arrest. Detective Chief Inspector Donald McDougall, one of the senior officers in the investigation, gave brisk evidence that when Robertson was cautioned and charged, his reply had been, "That, sir, is entirely wrong."

Chief Inspector McDougall told the court that when Robertson was searched, a rubber cosh was found in a pocket of his police uniform. A car with the registration number DYS 570 was found in a garage in Gorbals Street, and, when it was examined, there were traces of blood and hair on its underside.

From there on, so far as the Crown case was concerned, it was mainly a time for the technical experts, both mechanical and forensic, to begin their circumstantial evidence and tell of the inferences to be drawn from the car, from the markings found on the roadway, and from the dead woman's body.

At one stage, Lord Keith and the fifteen members of the jury followed the court macer out into a yard within the Justiciary Building. They inspected DYS 570, which was displayed on its side with timber props against its underside. Then it was back to the North Court, to more evidence of tests.

Traffic officers had taken the car out to Prospecthill Road and tried to reconstruct what had happened. Forensic experts told how they had crawled under the car and had used a girl volunteer to establish the pattern of injuries sustained by Catherine McCluskey and how they could have been caused. The girl concerned, a clerk from the Chief Constable's office, had been chosen because she was much the same build as the murdered woman.

For long hours the problem of exactly what had happened that night was investigated in fine focus as witnesses were examined by the Advocate Depute, then, in turn, closely cross-examined by the defence counsel.

Some tests, the witnesses concerned admitted, had been inconclusive. Others, however, had had more positive results.

Professor John Glaister, renowned son of a famous father and Regius Professor of Forensic Medicine at Glasgow University, had found no trace of blood on Robertson's uniform. The rubber truncheon had had a small stain which reacted to a presumptive test for blood, but that was not final proof that the stain was in fact blood.

When it came to the injuries suffered by the dead woman, he could be more certain. His opinion was that "the injuries were caused by a forward motion of the car going at some speed. I do not mean at a colossal speed, but I mean at some appreciable speed, and I think that that was done on more than one occasion."

He had found no injury on the woman's body or damage to the car which fitted the picture of her having been knocked down.

On the press bench, page after page in our notebooks was filled by the testimony of expert witnesses. Some of it was difficult to follow, other portions brutally clear. One theory put forward was that Robertson had first driven over the woman's body, then had turned the car round in the road and driven back over her again. There was much discussion of the reason why the exhaust pipe was broken. Had it been broken on the roadway – or against Catherine McCluskey's body?

At last, on the fifth day of the trial, the Crown case was concluded. The first witness called by the defence was the man at the centre of the drama.

James Ronald Robertson, who had been sitting with arms folded and head downcast, left the dock and, with an escort in close attendance, climbed the four steps into the witness-box. It was the first time there had been an opportunity to examine his appearance in any detail. He had lost weight. The blue lounge suit hung loose. Officers who knew him told me they reckoned that he had lost two stone in the period since his arrest.

The courtroom was packed, as it had been throughout. Many of those on the public benches were women. They had queued for hours every morning to be sure of a seat and some brought flasks and sandwiches. If anyone did leave the

building, there were always others outside wanting to take the
vacant seat.

In the witness-box, Robertson stood in an erect, disciplined
"at ease" position as he began his evidence, answering Mr
Cameron's questions in a low – at times almost inaudible –
voice.

First, he gave details of his personal history. He had been
a policeman for five years and had met Catherine McCluskey
one night in 1949 when he was called to a disturbance in a
house where she was living.

Mr Cameron: "Did you see Catherine McCluskey many
times after your first meeting with her?"

"I came across her many times since then," was Robertson's
reply.

He answered questions about the car.

No, he claimed, he hadn't stolen it. What had happened
was that he had seen it on some waste ground one early
morning when he was on his way home from night shift. It
was still there the next morning when he returned home, and
by then he knew it was a vehicle which had been reported
stolen. He hadn't reported that he knew where it was, and on
the third morning had "taken it for a run". Afterwards he had
prepared false number-plates and had used it regularly.

He denied breaking into the motor showroom and stealing
either the radio or the registration books. He claimed that he
had found them lying in a Gorbals backyard one night when
he was on patrol.

Then, in a hushed court, he began his version of what had
happened on the night Catherine McCluskey died.

He had, he agreed, met her by appointment. He had seen
her the previous night and she had told him she had been
locked out of her home.

She was waiting at a street corner when he drove up in the
car at ten minutes past eleven. She climbed aboard and asked
him to drive her to Neilston, a village on the outskirts of
Glasgow, where a friend might take her in. But Neilston was
fourteen miles away, and he was, at least in theory, on duty.
He told her it couldn't be done.

Catherine McCluskey began to cry and, as they were
stopped in a conspicious place, he had started the car and
driven around, eventually reaching Prospecthill Road, where

he turned the car round again. He told the woman he would have to get back to duty in Cumberland Street, and she argued with him. Robertson said he had stopped the car and, after a further discussion, Catherine McCluskey had got out, saying she wouldn't go back.

Then, he claimed, he had driven away for about a hundred yards before slowing and stopping. By then, he thought, she would have changed her mind. He reversed down the darkened road.

What happened next was a sudden increase in the exhaust note from the car, then a jarring. He braked, stopped, opened the driver's door, and made to get out.

Mr Cameron asked quietly, "When you did this, did you see something?"

In a voice little more than a whisper, Robertson replied, "I saw a face on the ground below, under the running-board."

By now there was absolute quiet in the courtroom. A woman cleared her throat and it sounded loud. Jurors leaned forward to follow the man's words as he told how he used his torch to see Catherine McCluskey's face. Her mouth, he declared, was wide open and seemed filled with blood.

"There was a movement of the body as if there was breath, then it stopped and the blood seemed to recede back into her mouth."

"Did you form any opinion at the time whether she was alive or dead?" asked his counsel.

"I was quite satisfied she was dead."

"Were you shocked by this?"

"I was, sir."

In long and grim detail Mr Cameron led Robertson step by step through the various attempts he claimed he had made to free Catherine McCluskey's body from underneath the car. He couldn't get her out, and was soon convinced that her clothing was entangled with the propellor-shaft. As Robertson told it, the scene was a nightmare.

By his own admission "panic stricken", he said he had eventually got back into the car, reversed it a little, tried again, then driven forward. At last the movement of the car had allowed him to get the body free.

He had sat in the driving seat for a few minutes, the body lying just behind the car. Afterwards, he had driven back to

Cumberland Street, stopping on the way to make a temporary repair to the broken exhaust. On arrival, he had resumed duty.

Now it was the Advocate Depute's turn. Mr Leslie began his cross-examination by asking, "Have you heard the evidence about a policeman paying certain money per week to Catherine McCluskey?"

"Yes."

"Do you know about that?"

"I know about it now."

"Were you the policeman?" asked Mr Leslie, in his rich, Orcadian voice.

"I certainly was not," declared Robertson. "I never was very friendly with her."

Mr Leslie turned to the car journey.

"You were getting about in a stolen car with that second evil, a woman, in it. It was a complicated situation?"

"It was a situation that could very easily become complicated," countered Robertson.

Moments later, Mr Leslie put one of the main issues squarely to the man in the witness-box. "Is it not the case that, before you got that woman out of the car, you struck her with a rubber truncheon?"

"No, certainly that is not the case." His voice low, Robertson still stuck by his answer to the charge of murder: "I reversed the car into Catherine McCluskey and killed her, but it was an accident."

After two hours and nineteen minutes, Robertson returned to his place in the dock. The rest of the defence evidence, in the main testimony from expert witnesses supporting the possibility of his version, lasted most of the next day, a Friday. The court adjourned for the weekend.

Over Saturday and Sunday the jury, secluded in a city hotel and supervised by court officials, had a break from their task.

Behind the scenes, members of the legal profession discussed an aspect of the trial which they found of unusual interest. It would have to be concluded by the Wednesday. There was no doubt of that now; even at an earlier stage there had been some concern over the possibility that the proceedings would over-run.

The Wednesday would be the hundred and tenth day to

pass since Robertson's committal, the deadline by which the case had to be completed under the Scottish Criminal Procedure Act.

Monday morning saw the same packed courtroom as first Mr Leslie and then Mr Cameron addressed the jury.

In one sentence, Mr Leslie presented a clear motive for the murder:

"I feel it incumbent upon me to submit that there was a bond between the two which the woman was maintaining and he was seeking to break."

Mr Cameron's address, which lasted for two and a half hours and was interrupted for a lunch break, was equally eloquent.

He told the jury, "You hold a set of scales. On the right there is a human life, Robertson's. On the left is the evidence. You must be convinced that these scales can really be tipped – theory, surmise or suspicion will not do. You have got to have proof."

And, referring to suggestions that Robertson was the father of the dead woman's child, he reminded the jury, "He is not being charged with that. The charge is murder."

Lord Keith summed up, and the jury retired. By then it was early evening, but few people on the public benches left their seats.

It was almost six o'clock, after an absence of an hour, when the jury returned to bring in a majority verdict of murder. Lord Keith pronounced sentence of death. As he finished and as the dock rail was opened, Robertson hurried down the stairs to the cells as if anxious to hide from the eyes around him.

A little later a police van drove him to prison. Police had to clear a passage for it through a crowd of hundreds waiting outside the Justiciary Buildings, a crowd who shouted, clapped and jeered as they caught a glimpse of a figure through the van's near-opaque glass.

An appeal was lodged and was dismissed. But even then, according to other prisoners, Robertson was still convinced that he wouldn't hang. He hoped for a last-minute reprieve. It was only in the last two or three days remaining to him that the truth of his situation penetrated.

On 16 December 1950, James Ronald Robertson was executed at Barlinnie Prison. A callous killer, he might have

escaped detection – if it hadn't been for the cautious, take-nothing-for-granted attitude of a traffic police constable who looked at a road accident, did not like what he saw, and started off such a widespread investigation.

Two Single-Horsepower Cases

(1)

The Hansom Hearse

The Reverend Evelyn Burnaby*

Sometime Rector of Burrough-on-the-Hill, Leicestershire, Evelyn Burnaby was a member of a family that claimed to be the oldest in that county. His mother lived to be over a hundred; one of his sisters, Mrs Manners-Sutton, was considered by many of her mid-nineteenth-century contemporaries to be the most beautiful woman of the age; his brother, Colonel Fred Burnaby, commander of a regiment of Horse Guards, was reckoned to be the strongest man in the British Army. (A pen-portrayer of Evelyn, speaking in passing of Fred, noted that he once "carried a pony under each arm up the stairs of the cavalry barracks at Windsor. . . . Colonel Burnaby made a successful trip in a balloon across the Channel – alone and with only a biscuit and a bottle of Apollinaris for sustenance.") The Reverend Evelyn explained that his fascination with criminal trials was seeded in his pre-Eton childhood, while he was living in Bedfordshire: "My first appearance in a Crown Court was at the Spring Assizes of 1856, when I was taken by my mother to hear three cases tried before Mr Justice Cresswell in the old Shire Hall, facing St Paul's Church, and

*adjoining the old Grammar School at
Bedford. It was here that Lord Brampton
[better known as Sir Henry Hawkins –
and still better known as "The Hanging
Judge"] was educated [also, for about
seven years till 1909, Ronald True – the
maniac who in 1922 murdered a London
prostitute whose business-name was Olive
Young]. From that moment I took a keen
interest in the law courts, and the
acquaintance of my family with my dear
old friend, Mr Justice Wightman, helped
to increase that interest. Many a time I
have sat by him when he was trying cases,
and as a lad I accompanied him on the
old Norfolk circuit. It was a pleasure to
me to attend the Old Bailey Sessions and
listen to the speeches of famous advocates
engaged on either side, and note the
gradual unfolding of the evidence – generally circumstantial – at the same time gath-
ering an insight into the extraordinary and
marvellous combination of good and evil
in the characters of real drama, for I have
never yet met a criminal in whom there
was not some inherent good."*

ABOUT TWO O'CLOCK on the afternoon of Saturday, 11
September 1875, a young man, hatless and breathless,
attracted considerable attention as he raced through London
streets after a four-wheeled cab. The latter stopped for a
moment in Greenfield Street [now Road], Whitechapel, and
picked up a woman, but before the young man could reach it,
it started off again. After it went the runner, and only once
did he check his speed. This was when he saw two policemen
in Leadenhall Street. Pulling up close to them, he said, "That
four-wheeler – quick – stop it, stop it – parcels - two parcels!"
The policemen looked at him and then laughed derisively.

The young man wasted no further time, but panted after
the cab again, following it over London Bridge, and at last
came up with it as it stopped near the Hop Exchange in the
Borough. Here there were two more policemen. This time he
had better luck. In gasping tones, just as a burly, bearded

man, smoking a big cigar and carrying a parcel, stepped from the vehicle, the runner said:

"Stop that man with that parcel! See where he goes with it! It's murder, I tell you! – murder!"

One of the constables at once followed the man in question while the other watched the cab.

Presently the bearded man, still smoking his cigar, came back to the four-wheeler empty-handed; and, without taking any notice of the policemen, lifted out the second parcel and walked off. This time, however, he was stopped. Both constables went up to him, and one said, "What's in that parcel? What have you done with the other one?" Then to his companion, "Go into the Hen & Chickens and see what it is, mate."

"Don't you do anything of the sort," said the man with the parcel. "You let me go. If £50 is any use to you, you can have the money at once."

The answer the policemen made to this was to suddenly pull aside the American-cloth covering of the parcel. In another instant he had signed to his companion, who seized the burly man from behind; there was a click of handcuffs and Henry Wainwright was a prisoner. At the same time they took into custody the other occupant of the four-wheeler. This was the woman who had been picked up in Greenfield Street. Her name was Alice Day; she was a dancer at the Pavilion Theatre in Whitechapel Road.

The man who had brought about the dramatic arrest was Alfred Philip Stokes. That morning he had been asked by Henry Wainwright, for whom he had formerly worked, to come with him to his old premises, 215[1] Whitechapel Road, to help him with two parcels and some other things. The two parcels, heavy, queer-shaped bundles, lay on the floor of the empty warehouse, wrapped in black American-cloth and corded across with strong rope. "They're too heavy for one to carry," said Stokes when Wainwright told him to pick them up. "All right," said his employer, "I'll give you a hand with them till we can get a cab."

So the two carried them as far as the church in the Whitechapel Road, Wainwright explaining on the way that they were

1. Premises in the road have been renumbered. 215 is now 130.

(left) 215 Whitechapel Road

parcels of bristles for brush-making that he had managed to
secrete from his creditors. At the church the parcels were
deposited on the pavement, Wainwright telling Stokes to mind
them while he went to look for a cab. Stokes was curious. The
weight of the parcels was altogether inconsistent with the story

that they contained bristles. Moreover, there was something about them that made him shudder. They gave off a strong, peculiar, offensive smell. He could not see any signs of Wainwright coming back, so he resolved to peep into one of them that had the wrapper slightly loose at one end.

He pulled the cloth aside and looked. To his horror he saw a human head covered with light hair, and behind it a human hand and the remains of an arm.

Dazed with the discovery, Stokes mechanically pulled the cloth over the parcel again, and just as he had done so, Wainwright drove up with the four-wheeler. He did not notice that the parcel had been disturbed, and said to Stokes, "Put the things in the cab, quick." In a mechanical way, Stokes did as he was bidden. Directly he had done so, Wainwright jumped into the vehicle, saying, "I'll see you at your place tonight. Commercial Road, cabby – sharp!" and the vehicle drove off.

It was not till he saw it moving away that Stokes realized what he had done. The significance of the affair came upon him like a flash, and he started off on the wild chase which had such a dramatic finish near the Hop Exchange in the Borough.

Directly Henry Wainwright was arrested, he was taken to the police station, together with the parcels. These were at once submitted to medical examination. One contained the trunk of a female body; the other the head and limbs – ten portions in all. It was evident that death had taken place about a year before, decay having been prevented by the action of chloride of lime, with which the remains were covered. The cause of death was abundantly clear. Two bullet wounds were in the brain, and in a hair-pad at the back of the head another flattened bullet was found.

The police were evidently in the presence of a great crime, and at once set to work to discover its details. With keys found on Wainwright when searched, and accompanied by Stokes, they went to 215 Whitechapel Road. Here in the great workshop and warehouse, a room 115 feet in length, they soon found further evidence. About twenty feet from the door, they noticed that some boards had lately been taken up and put down again. They removed them, and underneath there was an empty grave, the mould of which was thickly strewn with chloride of lime, such as was adhering to the fragments of the

Henry Wainwright

body in the parcels. In the grave three buttons were discovered. Other things found were a new spade recently used,
a chopper with some fleshy, evil-smelling matter adhering to
it, a pocket-knife open and with similar sticky fleshy matter
on it, a hammer, and an old blue parasol.

The first clue to the victim's identity was furnished four days
later, on 15 September 1875. Then a man named Taylor came
forward and said he believed the remains to be those of his
sister-in-law, Harriet Lane, with whom Wainwright had been
on terms of intimacy. She had been missing since 11 September

1874, twelve months to the day before Henry Wainwright was arrested. Taylor's description was minute, and when he saw the remains he at once identified them. So, too, did Mrs Taylor, the deceased woman's sister, and her father, John Lane. Harriet's connection with Wainwright was well known to her friends, and on the very day she was last seen alive she had informed them that she was going to 215 Whitechapel Road, to live there.

Three weeks later, having heard nothing of her sister, Mrs Taylor called on Wainwright to know "what was the matter with Harriet?" Wainwright told her that she had left him and had gone to Brighton with a man named Freake, who had come into a fortune. Two months later, Mrs Taylor was shown a telegraphic message from Dover, which stated that she (Harriet) was well and was leaving for France, and a day or two afterwards Wainwright read to her a letter purporting to come from Harriet, saying that she was enjoying herself with "a friend in Paris".

With Wainwright's arrest, these facts were recalled. The neighbours, too, began to recollect strange circumstances. One came forward to prove that on 10 November 1874, the day before the one on which the murder was committed, Wainwright had purchased a quantity of chloride of lime. Another proved by his books that on the same date the prisoner had bought a spade and an axe from him. Another, a girl named Pinnel, who lived near 215 Whitechapel Road, recollected hearing shots fired.

Facts were indeed strong against the accused man, and grew still stronger when it was proved that the telegram from Dover and the letter from Paris were both sent by Henry Wainwright's brother Thomas. The latter was promptly arrested as an accessory to the murder after the fact, and, with his brother, was committed for trial. The woman, Alice Day, had been previously discharged, there being nothing whatever to connect her with the crime.

There are a few interesting details which should not be omitted in regard to this sensational case. To account for the disappearance of Harriet Lane, letters were received by her family from a Mr Freake, saying she had gone away with him and was perfectly happy. These were proved to be in the handwriting of Thomas Wainwright. I had the opportunity of seeing the letters and learnt a lesson in the art of identifying handwriting. It was not so much in the formation of the letters that the similarity of Thomas Wainwright's handwriting with that in the letters was established, but the manner in which one letter was joined to another; the way the letter "o" was connected to the next one was very peculiar – a line being drawn up from the extreme bottom part of the "o" to the top of the letter succeeding.

Another circumstance worth noting is that when Harriet Lane left her home the last time she was seen alive, she made a statement as to where she was going. This evidence was not admissible against the prisoner as he was not present when it was made; only a statement made by a dying person, who is beyond all hope of recovery, is admissible against a prisoner who was elsewhere. The judge, whilst refusing to admit the evidence, pointed out to the jury that Harriet walked away carrying her nightdress in her bag, therefore she was going to spend the night somewhere, and when she left her home she proceeded in the direction of the house of the prisoner at the bar. In connection with dying declarations, I would refer to a remarkable case, Regina v. Butcher. A man was shot through a glass window, the prisoner being outside; before the bullet reached him the flash of the gun revealed to him the face of his assailant and he cried out as he was meeting his fate, "There's Butcher." This was admitted as evidence by the judge who tried the case – not as a dying declaration but as part of the res gestae, or part of the act of the crime.

The trial of Henry and Thomas Wainwright, which lasted nine days, commenced at the Old Bailey on 22 November, and ended on 1 December, 1875. Lord Chief Justice Cockburn made a point of specially going down to the court to try the case. After Sir John Holker, the Attorney-General, had completed the case for the Crown, Mr Besley (for Henry Wainwright) proceeded to open the defence. Lord Chief Justice Cockburn asked whether he would prefer that he should interrupt him in the course of his speech with any points of difficulty which suggested themselves to his mind, so that counsel for the prisoner might clear them up as he went along. Mr Besley, having expressed his assent, had not got very far with his address when he invited the jury to come to the conclusion that it was a case of suicide. I shall never forget his

Lord Chief Justice Cockburn

look of horror when Lord Chief Justice Cockburn, with that quiet manner which was peculiar to him, leaned over towards counsel and remarked: "and buried herself."

During the course of the trial, I noticed that the Lord Chief Justice was making notes to form the basis of his summing-up to the jury, and I had the curiosity, on passing his chair during one of the adjournments for luncheon, to look over the first sheet of the notes. I read as follows:

"Henry Wainwright found in possession of a body." . . . "*Dead body*." "Dead body *mutilated*." "*Dead body recently disinterred*"; and then the further suggestive remark which he repeated to the jury, "Man found in possession of stolen property shortly after it is stolen presumed to be the thief. Man found in the possession of a body evidently murdered presumed to be the murderer, unless he can give a reasonable account of how he became possessed of it."

Both prisoners were convicted – Henry Wainwright of murder, and Thomas Wainwright of being an accessory after the fact, the latter receiving a sentence of seven years' penal servitude.

As the two prisoners were in the dock awaiting the verdict of the jury, Henry Wainwright said to Thomas (the conversation was repeated to me afterwards by the chief warder): "They will convict me, Tom, and they will let you off. I shall say that you did it." Thomas replied, "You are the biggest murderer unhung – but that will not be for very long, for you will be hung."

On their return to the gaol – and this I am able to vouch for on the information of the governor – Thomas Wainwright sent for Mr Sydney Smith, who then controlled Newgate, and asked him to obtain from his brother information as to the exact hour when the murder was committed. This was done. "Now," said Thomas, "go to my employer and get the workbook, and you will find that on that day and at that time I was engaged nine miles away from the premises where the crime was committed."

Throughout the trial, Henry Wainwright maintained the utmost composure. For years he had been a prominent member of the Christ Church Institute in the East End, and had made himself popular by helping at religious meetings, and by giving recitations and amateur dramatic performances in aid of various charities. Yet it was shown that these things were merely the cover to a career of unbounded immorality and profligacy.

He was nonchalant to the last. Just before his execution, on 21 December 1875, he confessed that his fate was deserved, though he declared he was not wholly guilty of the deed for which he was to suffer. On the eve of his execution, at his special request, he was allowed a cigar. This he smoked in the prison yard, walking up and down with Mr Smith, the governor, boasting to the latter in the most cynical way "that no woman could resist him".

Though Wainwright's execution was supposed to be private, over sixty persons were admitted by the sheriffs to witness it. Major Arthur Griffiths, who was officially present, says: "He came gaily out of his cell, nodded pleasantly to the governor, who stood just opposite, and then walked briskly to the execution shed, smiling as he went along. There was a smile

on his face when it was last seen, just as the terrible white cap
was drawn over it."

(2)

The Wicked Hansom

Edmund Pearson

IT WAS SAD that hansom-cabs should fall under a blight. A
curse descended upon them in 1904. Although they were jolly,
teetery-looking carriages, and more innocent than your limou-
sines, pious folk thought of them, for many years, as chariots
of sin.

The notorious hansom which disgraced all its tribe in New
York was driven by Frederick Michaels, and the black hour
came upon him on the fair morning of Saturday, 4 June 1904.
The time was as early as half-past seven – when the wicked
have usually gone to bed, and the virtuous are abroad.
Michaels and his horse belonged with the good and the pure,
and so they were looking for business in Columbus Circle,
while the dew was still on the grass in Central Park.

A man and a girl hailed the cab. They got in; the hansom
turned, I suppose, through 59th Street, and started down Fifth
Avenue.

The only noise it made was the familiar cloppety-clop of
the horse's hooves on the asphalt. But if Michaels had been
endowed with second-sight – no, with second-hearing – he
would have detected the Fates, or some other sinister crea-
tures, muttering the soon-to-be notorious names of "Miss-
Nan-Patterson-and-Caesar-Young . . .   Miss-Nan-Patterson-
and- Caesar-Young".

And, as an accompanying chorus of doom, like the
unpleasant old busybodies in a Greek tragedy, the grumbling
voices of half a dozen New York clergymen, who were very
shortly to be repeating the names of the man and the girl, and
adding: "The-wages-of-sin-is-certainly-death . . . the-wages-
of-sin-is-certainly-death."

Nan Patterson

Ann Elizabeth Patterson, a fatally beautiful lady of twenty-two, was a native of the city of Washington. Newspapers said that three men had already died – absolutely perished and crossed the dark river – for love of her. From her sixteenth to her twentieth year she had been the wife of a railroad official named Martin, but she secured a divorce in 1903.

Her real celebrity, up to the moment she entered this hansom, lay in the fact that she was a "Floradora girl". As it is said to be a scientific fact that when "the original Floradora double sextette" – i.e., twelve persons – held a reunion in Pittsburgh, it took five hotels to accommodate them, we must enquire into Nan Patterson's exact status in that vast chorus. Good authorities say that she belonged to the second sextette, organized by Edna Wallace Hopper in 1901.

On a westbound train, before her divorce, Nan Patterson

met Frank T. Young, called "Caesar". Mr Young, an Englishman, had come to America, years earlier, to compete in
track and field athletics for the Manhattan Athletic Club. He
married; fell upon hard times; took up book-making at Morris
Park track, where he prospered greatly – sometimes as a result
of the excellent advice of his wife, who was a good judge of
horses. He was said to possess $750,000. In his pocket, as he
sat in the cab, were $1,820 and two tickets on the SS *Germanic*,
sailing for Europe that morning at ten o'clock.

The second ticket was not for Miss Patterson, but for Mrs
Young, then waiting on, or near, the ship. She was patiently
and tolerantly hoping that her husband's promise to sail with
her indicated the end of his affair with "that Patterson
woman".

Early in the morning, Miss Patterson had been called by
telephone at the St Paul Hotel in 60th Street, where she lived
with her sister and brother-in-law, the J. Morgan Smiths.
Caesar Young bade her meet him at the 59th Street station of
the 6th Avenue "El". This she did, and she is the only witness
to most of the events which followed, for the cabman remained
more aloof than the gods upon Olympus.

It was, by her account, a bibulous ride. Caesar had already
been drinking when she met him. They had a drink together
before taking the cab. On the way down the Avenue, Caesar
discussed his old hat, and the universal opinion that he needed
a new one. At Knox's, in Madison Square, he alighted and
bought a new hat. In Bleecker Street – they were on their way
towards the pier – he demanded another drink. They had
this, and when they were once more in the cab, Caesar was
melancholy, affectionate, and despairing, by turns.

"Are you going to leave me? Or are you going to follow
me to Europe?"

The girl replied:

"I am not going to Europe."

She went on: "When he grabbed hold of me, and kissed me
roughly, I pulled away from him . . . there was a flash, and
he was dead."

She added: "I never saw the pistol."

This happened in West Broadway, near Franklin Street.
Michaels was at last made aware that something was going on.

He drew up to the curb; a policeman came, and found Miss Patterson kissing her companion's face, as his head lay in her lap. Caesar never spoke, but died five minutes after reaching the hospital.

Whose was the pistol? Where did it come from? Which hand pulled the trigger? No jury which tried Miss Patterson for murder ever found an answer to these questions.

The defence steadily maintained that "Caesar" Young, in profound melancholy at the impending separation from his sweetheart, or from a recent loss of $30,000 on the track, or from drink, or from all three causes, held the pistol under his coat and shot himself.

The prosecution's theory was that Nan Patterson had been urged to the slaughter by J. Morgan Smith, who feared that she was losing a wealthy friend. The evidence by which they sought to bolster up this doubtful idea failed them altogether. (How would it profit her to kill him?) The ownership of the pistol was not satisfactorily traced to anybody. But for eleven months, the sob-sisters and the Sunday newspapers continued to discuss the beautiful defendant, her affairs, and her venerable father, while the country at large had a good time deploring the wickedness of New York.

Rural communities righteously thanked God that as they had no Floradora girls and no hansom-cabs, therefore they had no wayward husbands and no violent deaths.

The first trial was stopped by the illness of a juror. At the second trial the jury disagreed – six to six. At the third trial there was another disagreement, seven to five for acquittal, and the prisoner was discharged.

Miss Patterson's subsequent career upon the stage, in Pennsylvania, was brief and unsuccessful. Her later life, as a happily married woman on the Pacific coast, is said to have brought her the esteem of her neighbours. It is a pleasure to record this, since, if I may venture an opinion, she deserved an acquittal. The government's theory that she *plotted* to commit the crime seems all but destroyed by the fact that the meeting, that morning, was not the result of her arrangement.

We know the fate of some of the participants in that early-morning drive down the Avenue. The horse, in the natural course of things, dropped dead. But what became of the cabman and the hansom itself? Properly stuffed and mounted, they could well form an important exhibit in the Museum of the City of New York. As one of the most famous vehicles in our history, the cab deserves a place beside Boss Tweed's fire-engine, with the Tammany Tiger on it.

The Case of the Equivocal Cabbie

The Hon. H. Fletcher Moulton

THE STORY OF the murder of Jacob Dickey is one into which Romance enters not at all. Whoever did the deed committed a foul and dastardly crime, and committed it for the most sordid motives.

Whoever? – that is where the interest lies and why the story of the trial still lives. For the case is one of those which leaves a doubt whether, though every form of the Law was scrupulously observed, Justice was in fact done. And that doubt has been greatly strengthened by certain facts which subsequently came to light, and whose true significance seems never to have been appreciated. A twofold problem is therefore presented for the reader's verdict: firstly, was Alexander Campbell Mason the man who committed the crime for which he was sentenced, and secondly, is our English system quite so fair to the accused as most of us believe?

The murder for which Mason stood his trial was committed at about a quarter to ten on the evening of Wednesday, 9 May 1923, in Bay Tree Road, a turning off Acre Lane, one of the main east-to-west thoroughfares of south-west London. Of the beginning of the tragedy nothing is known with certainty. The actual story of the passers-by in Acre Lane tells only of two figures – mere silhouettes in the semi-darkness – seen struggling near a taxi-cab some forty yards down Bay Tree Road. One cries for help, "He's killing me! Save me! save me!" – the other throws him to the ground, and, crouching over him fires twice, then flings down the revolver and vanishes into the darkness, whilst his victim slowly rises and staggers towards the main road – but, as the onlookers press forward to help him, calls on them to go back, doubtless as a warning that his assailant is armed. And these are his last words, for at the corner of Acre Lane he collapses, and dies within the minute.

A beastly and a brutal murder – and an impudent murder too, considering the time and place of its commission. The sort of murder we read of in Chicago – and then take a sip from our glass and thank God we are not as the Americans are, and that that kind of thing couldn't happen in London. And yet, but for that innate and providential stupidity of the criminal, which is the greatest safeguard of the peaceful citizen, the assassin could probably have escaped undetected, and the murder have been classed amongst London's unsolved mysteries.

Certainly he could have escaped for the moment, and without any risk of identification. Bay Tree Road lay open, and none sought to pursue him – one of the two witnesses was seeking the police, whilst the other was engaged in stopping an omnibus that threatened to run down the dying man. A minute's run would have taken the murderer into Brixton Hill and comparative safety.

Neither of the two eye-witnesses saw the beginning of the struggle, and it is a curious feature of the case that, though each spoke of hearing screams or moans before arriving at the corner of Bay Tree Road, neither had heard any shots, though the evidence shows that four must have been fired before they arrived on the scene.

The criminal or criminals had departed before any constable arrived, but he or they had left material from which the police could start their investigations. On the pavement by the cab was a walking-stick of somewhat unusual pattern, whilst in the roadway nearer Acre Lane were a revolver, a blood-stained suede glove and a jemmy wrapped in paper. The taxi-meter of the cab, examined soon after the tragedy, marked five shillings and threepence as the fare.

Further investigations showed the route which had been taken by a man who had apparently been concerned in the crime. A torch was found in the garage yard of 28 Bay Tree Road, and from further discoveries of footprints, broken trellis-work, marks on walls, etc., a track was established leading through the garden of 33 Acre Lane, reappearing further down in No. 23 and apparently continuing to No. 15[1].

The next evidence was that of two ladies living at No. 15

1. See exhibits on pages 149 and 150.

Bury Turn Road (page from a two Lane)

Acre Lane, who stated that at about a quarter to ten they heard their dog barking in the back garden, and that on going out one of them found a man on the wall, who asked if he could go through the house. They let him through, and beyond the fact that one of them said jokingly that "It must have been the burglars", seemed to pay very little attention to the matter, till the police called later in the evening with the news of the murder. On the afternoon of the next day a little girl found a glove in the garden of 25 Acre Lane which proved to be the fellow of that found near the taxi-cab.

The police were also able to ascertain that Jacob Dickey had come from a rank near the Trocadero, Piccadilly Circus, which he had left about 9 p.m., and from the reading on the clock would appear to have gone straight to Bay Tree Road. There was no reason to suppose that he had any criminal associates or special enemies, or that he was anything but an ordinary hardworking cabman. There seemed, therefore, no prospect of starting any fruitful line of investigation from the history or associations of the murdered man, and the only chance of discovering the criminal lay in the identification of one or more of the articles found at the scene of the crime.

A photograph of the stick was inserted in the papers on the Friday following the murder, and produced immediate information, with the result that at eight o'clock on Saturday morning the police went to a house in Charlwood Street, Pimlico, and found a man and a woman – James Vivian and Hettie Colquhon – who were taken to Brixton Police Station. There Vivian made a statement which led to the arrest of Mason about eight o'clock in the evening.

On the next day – Sunday – Vivian and Mason, together with eleven other men, were paraded for identification by Miss Trebel and Miss Bliss, through whose house the man had passed on the night of the murder. Both women said they thought Mason was the man, though neither seemed very certain.

Mason was charged with the murder at Brixton Police Court, and after a number of adjournments was committed for trial. The jury at the inquest on Jacob Dickey also returned a verdict charging him with the murder. The most remarkable feature of these preliminary proceedings was the almost complete silence maintained by the prisoner.

Mason was committed for trial at the Old Bailey, where the Grand Jury found a True Bill against him, and on 11 July he was charged with the murder on their indictment, and also on the Coroner's inquisition, to which charges he pleaded Not Guilty. The trial took place before Mr Justice Rigby Swift, Sir Richard Muir leading for the Prosecution and Mr Fox-Davies for the Defence.

In the story as told at the trial, all the principal actors were moving within the criminal world, or at least uncomfortably close to its borders, and the value of their evidence must be estimated rather from its consonance or dissonance with ordinary probability and the undisputed facts than from any fancied value given to it by the sanctity of the oaths they had taken.

Alexander Campbell Mason[2] was twenty-two years of age at the time of his trial. He had been born at Omea in Lanarkshire, Scotland, and after the death of his father, his mother went to Canada, where she remarried, leaving the boy with his grandparents at Motherwell. In some way, however, Mason too had gone to Canada, either before or during the Great War. There he had joined the Canadian Navy, deserted from the service, and, whilst still a deserter, broken into a shop and been convicted and sentenced to three years' penal servitude. After serving twenty months of this sentence, he was deported to his native country, and was taken to live with his grandparents in Lanarkshire, a kindness which he repaid by committing burglary in his grandfather's house and decamping to London. In July 1921, he was convicted at the County of London Sessions, but released under the Probation Act; he was again convicted of burglary in January 1922, and after serving his sentence was re-arrested and taken to Scotland, where he was charged, convicted and sentenced to six months' imprisonment for the theft from his grandfather's house.

He was released from prison on the morning of Saturday, 5 May 1923, and that night travelled to King's Cross. On his arrival in London he walked across to the Blackfriars Road to see an old friend, one Daniel Nunn, who gave him breakfast and, what he more particularly needed, the address of another old comrade, James or "Eddie" Vivian.

2. The prisoner was also known as "Scottie", or "Scottie Munroe".

Alexander Campbell Mason

Vivian was a man of about the same age as Mason and with a record no more creditable. He openly admitted not only his recorded convictions, but the fact that his only regular occupation was housebreaking; the sole hint in the whole of his evidence that he had any sense of moral values was that

Eddie Vivian

he preferred that it should be thought that the rent and living expenses of his household were procured by means of burglary rather than from the immoral earnings of the woman with whom he lived – though it is more than doubtful if the ethical scruples thus displayed were in fact carried into practical effect.

He was an old friend of Mason's – perhaps it were better

to say an old workmate, as they had done a number of little jobs together, for one of which they had been jointly convicted in January 1922; though on that occasion Vivian had received a stiffer sentence than Mason, by reason of being found with a revolver, he had come out of prison some months before the latter, since Mason had also had to serve his Scotch sentence.

But Vivian had not been unmindful of his less fortunate comrade. Shortly before the date of Mason's release, he had written to him asking him to come to London, and saying that he had work for him there. In view, however, of the letter being subject to the inspection of the Scottish prison officials, he had modestly signed himself "Uncle", and had apparently given the address of their mutual friend, Daniel Nunn. Nor had he confined himself to mere words and promises, for although he had had no employment whatever since leaving prison, Vivian had found the means to send the prisoner clothing and £2 in cash. Can anyone wonder that Mason on his release should at once seek so staunch a friend?

Mr and Mrs Vivian – née Hettie Colquhon, and still in the sight of the law entitled to bear that name, since the marriage ceremony had been omitted – were at this time living at 34 Charlwood Street, Pimlico. Their living apartment consisted of but a single room on the second floor, for which they paid the not inconsiderable rent of 22s. per week. The household, however, possessed advantages for a gentleman of Vivian's profession, since the proprietress lived at the back of the house, and it was possible to enter and leave without disturbing or being observed by their landlady.

Hettie Colquhon plays little active part in this drama. Her rôle was chiefly that of a spectator – probably a rather sad and anxious spectator, for though she asked no imprudent questions, she was clearly aware of her lover's record and occupation, and tried to persuade him to forgo the dangerous profits he sought. She described herself as a chorus girl, although her only earnings from that employment in the year in question had been in an engagement at Belfast in January at a salary of £3 per week. Yet she disappeared each evening, and the rent was paid somehow, and the household expenses too – and there was a surplus to help a fallen brother.

Pathetic figures, the Hettie Colquhons. The presence or absence of that virtue named chastity does not of necessity determine the whole nature of woman – nor does the omission of the marriage ceremony relieve her from anxiety and fear for her man. If Hettie's testimony were biased in favour of her lover, who should blame her, remembering the dreadful fate that probably awaited the loser in the duel of oaths.[3]

At ten o'clock on Sunday morning, Mason arrived at Charlwood Street, and was entertained there for the rest of the day. Hettie went out to purchase the breakfast, and subsequently they all three had dinner and tea together. In the afternoon the two men went out walking – the lady being left behind – but apparently Mason's appearance was not sufficiently fashionable for Vivian's taste, and he therefore lent him a stick and a pair of gloves to add to his dignity. On Monday, Tuesday and Wednesday, Mason returned and spent the greater part of the day with Vivian, partly at Charlwood Street and partly in various excursions through London.

But it was soon made clear to Mason that it was not intended that he should eat the bread of idleness. Vivian's letter had said that there was work for him to do in London, and no time was wasted in starting thereon. On Monday or Tuesday – there is a dispute as to which – exploratory expeditions were made in the direction of the Crystal Palace in order to choose a suitable house for a burglary, and necessary implements in the shape of a jemmy and an electric torch were purchased.

It may seem strange that a person of Vivian's avowed occupation should need to purchase a jemmy, and the explanation shows the spread of business principles even to the humble profession of burglary. To be found at night with a jemmy is a serious matter, especially if you have already been convicted of a felony, and the skilful craftsman takes no unnecessary risks. Vivian knew of a shop where one could buy jemmies[4] at 1s. 3d. apiece, and their cheapness, as he explained to Mason, enabled him to halve the risk by throwing the jemmy away as soon as its work was finished, and so make the return journey unhampered by so dangerous an article.

3. I will say at once that there was no proof of such bias, but it will be necessary later to consider possibilities involving a criticism, or at least a disregard, of some of Hettie Colquhon's evidence.
4. "Jemmy" is simply the slang term for a case-opener – an instrument which has many perfectly legitimate uses, and can therefore be freely purchased.

Another practical precaution, which he also impressed upon Mason, was that on such expeditions a walking-stick should invariably be carried, as it lent an air of innocence, and so served as a shield against the suspicions of their enemies the police – a maxim which, as circumstances fell out, had the most tragic consequences.

Both men were amazingly frank about their conduct on these expeditions, in which, according to Mason's account, Vivian usually adopted the rôle of watcher, allowing his comrade to do the actual burglary (but we are not given Vivian's version on this point).

So far, I have confined myself to uncontroverted evidence to show the general setting of the scene before the tragedy itself. It is now necessary to consider the stories told for the Prosecution and Defence, and the divergencies between them.

The first controversy arose on the question as to whether Mason was in possession of a revolver. Vivian's story on this point is that shortly before his release Mason had managed to get a letter smuggled out of prison and delivered to Vivian, asking him to procure a revolver. This note he said he had destroyed – which was not unnatural in the circumstances.[5]

In consequence he had been to see their friend Nunn the day before Mason arrived in London, in order to make the necessary arrangements, and on the Monday morning he and Mason met Nunn at a public house in the Blackfriars Road, when the delivery of the revolver was promised. On the same evening Mason met Nunn again in the Waterloo Road, and when later Vivian joined them there he was told by one or the other that the revolver had been supplied.[6]

Mason and Vivian then went to Crane's Restaurant, 248 Westminster Bridge Road, where Mason produced the revolver and loaded it from a large match-box containing some twenty-five cartridges, and then said that he felt inclined to use it to "stick up" a taxi-driver and take his money. Vivian in reply told him not to be a fool, but apparently did not then

5. See, however, page 166.
6. Vivian's statement on this point differed somewhat from that which he gave at the trial.

take the threat seriously. Subsequently the two went for a walk in the direction of Euston.

Mason denied the whole story. He had sent no note to Vivian, nor had he ever tried to get a revolver from Nunn or anyone else. It was true that they had met Nunn – though this was on the Tuesday, not the Monday, morning – but it was a mere friendly visit with no ulterior motive, and they did not see Nunn again. What in fact they did on the Monday evening was to purchase a jemmy, and then prospect in the direction of the Crystal Palace – a journey which they repeated the next night.

But Mason's evidence was not wholly negative – he too had a tale of a revolver, and like Vivian's it had a prelude before the weapon actually appeared. His story was that, when he went to Nunn on first arriving in London, Nunn had warned him against Vivian, saying that the latter had been worrying him for some time to get him a revolver for his own use, but that he had refused to do so. Then, on going to Charlwood Street on Monday morning, Mason had found Vivian in bed, and in the course of dressing, whilst Hettie was out purchasing the breakfast, Vivian had produced a revolver from his coat pocket, and a handful of cartridges from the pocket of his waistcoat, whereupon Mason had told him that he would not work with him if he carried a revolver. Vivian had then gone out of the room, and on returning had said that, as the revolver and cartridges might come in useful sometime, he had put them on the top of the flush cistern in the lavatory – a hiding-place of which more will be heard.[7]

There are points about each story which invite criticism. It seems difficult to believe that a prisoner on the eve of his discharge would take the risk of writing and sending such a dangerous message as Vivian described, or that Mason would produce and load a revolver whilst sitting in an eating-house. On the other hand, Mason's story implies that Vivian habitually carried the revolver and cartridges on him – a dangerous course for anyone, especially an ex-convict. One point is, however, established – that Vivian either went armed himself,

---

7. Fifteen cartridges were subsequently found there, which at first sight seems a bulky load for a waistcoat pocket, but in fact such a pocket will hold this number easily.

or was quite ready and willing to work with an armed accomplice.

Each of these stories hinged round Nunn, who merits a few words. An old Army man, Nunn, with seventeen years' service to his credit, lived on his pension and what he described as a little second-hand dealing. There was nothing against him in Police Records, but if a man is to be judged by his friends, Nunn had not been lucky in his choice. His evidence completely supported Mason's version, and he denied emphatically that he had supplied the weapon with which the murder was committed. But whilst it is a witness's business to give evidence, it is for the judge and jury to assess its value – and it is clear from the judge's summing up and the jury's verdict that they placed that value at nil[8].

Returning for a moment to the murder itself, it will be remembered that one of the articles found was a somewhat peculiar walking-stick. Inquiries of the maker showed that only a few dozen of this particular pattern had been sold, and no doubt the purchaser could have been traced, but this would have been of little help, for undoubtedly the stick had at some time been stolen from its original owner[9]. Any long investigations were, however, unnecessary, for some person identified it as Vivian's property[10], but it still might have been difficult to prove that it was so in fact, for such informants usually desire to remain unknown, and it is the practice of the police to respect their desires – otherwise the number of unsolved mysteries would be increased many thousand per cent[11]. But this trouble was spared them by Vivian admitting ownership, and telling a story that led to his becoming the principal witness for the prosecution.

According to this story, Vivian had daily supplied Mason

8. Clearly, too, Nunn had a grudge against Vivian, whom he believed to have informed the police that he was a receiver of stolen goods.
9. Vivian's own account was that he had purchased it in a public house some weeks previously.
10. Sir Richard Muir put to Mason in cross-examination that a man Hook, who had visited him in prison, had told him that the stick had been identified by one "Chinkey-eyed" Len – a gentleman with whom Vivian had had a fight in which the said stick figured prominently. But when Hook subsequently went into the box he denied having said this, and professed ignorance of the identity of the informant.
11. The Scotland Yard Police Code contained the direction that "where information is given under a promise of confidence, the promise must be strictly respected".

with small sums of money, but by the Wednesday his resources had come to an end[12]. Obviously the time had come to replenish the joint exchequer by performing some of that work for which Mason had been summoned to London. But though the spirit was willing, the flesh was weak – Vivian was not feeling well, and was, as he believed, suffering from some form of ptomaine poisoning, which he attributed to a tin of sardines he had eaten on the Sunday.

The symptoms gradually grew more distressing, and though he was able to indulge in extensive perambulations – partly on business and partly on pleasure – on the Monday and Tuesday, and even to walk out in the afternoon of Wednesday, by the evening he was incapable of any effort, and had been compelled to take to his bed, so that at half-past seven Mason had gone off alone, leaving Vivian and Hettie Colquhon at Charlwood Street. And he had not gone empty-handed: remembering Vivian's precepts as to the necessity of a smart appearance, he had taken a pair of gloves and a stick, together with the jemmy and torch for business purposes.

Vivian's wardrobe was severely limited as regards the more essential articles – he had in fact no other suit than that which he wore daily. But it was richer in luxuries or adornments, since it included at least two pairs of gloves and two walking-sticks. One of these latter was a plain affair with a bone handle, and it was this which he had lent his friend for the Sunday afternoon promenade. It did not, however, please Mason, who said it was an old man's stick and made him look ridiculous, and therefore on the Wednesday evening he had, according to Vivian, borrowed the more ornate gold-capped article.

This happens at 7.30, whilst Vivian is sitting half-undressed over the fire. At 8.30 Hettie departs on her nightly business and he lies down and sleeps, to be awakened at eleven – he notes the time particularly – by a rattling at the window and a whistle from the street below.

12. Mason only admitted borrowing a few shillings from Vivian. He stated that he had £3 when he arrived in London – Vivian had sent him £2 and he would have drawn money on leaving prison. He had laid out 9s. 6d. on boot repairs, and had paid for three nights' lodging, but seems to have had few other expenses. It must be remembered, however, that on the Monday afternoon he had been out with a lady-friend – which may have considerably depleted his resources.

It is Mason – bedraggled and dusty – with wounded hand and bloodstained clothing. And charged with terrible news – he has made a mess of things and shot a taxi-driver at Brixton. He gives details – horribly realistic – complains of the shocking inefficiency of the revolver – but for which he might have committed multiple murders – tells the story of his escape through the house – of the women's remark that "it was the burglars". He is under no illusions as to what the end will be – it means the rope for him – but what does it matter so long as he gets plenty to eat whilst awaiting his fate?

Vivian asks after his stick and is told that it and everything else has been left behind. He remarks sarcastically that that looks all right for him, and is assured by Mason that he will not be allowed to suffer – an assurance which apparently carries little conviction. But for the moment Vivian is troubled with more immediate matters. Hettie will be back soon and the tale is not one "for the ear of an innocent girl". An attempt is made to render Mason presentable, and a story prepared of a mythical fight with Jews – the incidents of which are probably inspired by one of Vivian's own experiences.

Hettie arrives, listens sympathetically, lends Mason a bandage for his wounded hand, and dispenses coffee. Mason begs to be allowed to stay the night, is given a rug and bidden to sleep in a chair or on the floor. But there is no sleep for him. Gone is all his bravado, and he paces the floor till the dawn – a dawn which brings fresh anxiety.

At seven o'clock Mason begs a penny, buys a paper, and, returning, points to an item which the two men read and discuss in whispers, lest they wake the sleeping girl. And Mason congratulates himself as he reads the news, for it tells that his victim had died without speaking.

Later in the morning, Hettie Colquhon lends Mason a needle. She has no black cotton and Mason cannot wait, so he pulls out the thread that binds the fringe of the tablecloth, and with it mends the rents in his clothing. Then he departs to visit his friend Nunn, and returns with better attire – a shirt without bloodstains and trousers newly pressed.

That night he sleeps at the house of another friend – one Reggie or Robert Hook – to return to Charlwood Street on Friday morning. But by now the hunt is on – the picture of the stick is in the papers, and Mason is a dangerous guest. He is bidden to come no more to the house, though an appointment is made to meet outside at eight o'clock. But Mason does not keep it – and Vivian next sees him in the dock.

Thus Vivian's story; now to hear Mason's.

On one point he agreed with Vivian, viz. as to the shortage of money, admitting that by Wednesday morning he himself was penniless, whilst Vivian only had five shillings, out of which several rounds of drinks were provided. Nor did he deny that it was proposed to abate that shortage by felonious means.

But Hettie Colquhon had become an obstacle to this. She had seen the jemmy on the dressing-table and had begged Vivian not to risk a burglary – who knew what she might do if she caught them starting on an expedition? Therefore it was resolved that to allay her suspicions Vivian should feign illness. His first complaint was made on Tuesday, and by Wednesday evening he professed himself fit only for bed – and how could the girl anticipate that a man in such a state would go a-burgling? So Mason left him to play the invalid till Hettie went out on her nightly business, and then rejoin him near Victoria.

Vivian arrived at the rendezvous about 8.30, equipped with stick, gloves, torch and jemmy. All plans had been made, and these included the use of a "straight-up" taxi, i.e. one whose driver was willing to join in criminal expeditions. Vivian said he knew of such a man, who usually stood on the rank at the Trocadero, and immediately took a ticket at Victoria for Piccadilly to pick him up, refusing to let Mason accompany him for fear the taxi-man should be suspicious if he saw a strange face before he was thoroughly instructed in the business. A rendezvous was accordingly arranged in Bay Tree Road, Brixton – their expedition was to be towards Tulse Hill. Mason was first to call at Nunn's to get some ready money – probably for paying the taxi – and then get to Bay Tree Road as best he could.

At Victoria they had chanced to meet one Jerry – whose full name was not given in Court – and Mason had a drink with him, before starting to walk to Webber Row, off the Waterloo Road, where Nunn lived. There he was told by Mrs Nunn that her husband had just gone out, but that he might catch him if he were quick. Time, however, did not allow for this, and he went straight on to Bay Tree Road.

Arrived there, he waited at the bend of the road, somewhere near No. 28, till the taxi drove up from Brixton Hill and the driver gave the prearranged signal – two long blasts of the horn followed by a short one. Mason stepped out to meet the cab, but it passed him and stopped some thirty or forty yards on. As the cab stopped, a man jumped out of the right-hand door, and the driver grabbed at his collar and was pulled half out of his seat. Then followed two reports and two flashes and both men fell, but rose again, locked together.

All this time Mason had been walking towards the cab till, when he was about fifteen yards from it, a third flash lighted the men's faces and showed that one was Vivian[13].

It was too much for Mason's nerves, and he turned and fled, climbing first into the garden of No. 28, then into its garage yard, and finally on to the high fence on the left of the yard. And then Vivian arrived, stumbling and falling, and crying for help because he could not run.

He scrambled somehow over the gates into the garage yard[14], and Mason helped him up on to the fence, both falling together into the open ground beyond. Mason was up at once, but Vivian did not move, and his companion went back to help, then heard the police whistles and ran off leaving him there.

Mason then climbed on to the wall running at the backs of the houses in Bay Tree Road[15] and followed it down to the end, near No. 2 Bay Tree Road, then jumped into the garden of No. 23 Acre Lane, crossed to the wall between 23 and 21 and went up that wall till he reached the backs of the houses in Acre Lane, turning right-handedly, climbed from garden to garden, seeking an opening to the street. In the yard of Craig's Warehouse (No. 17) he found a barrel from which he took a drink, and then climbed on to the back wall and tried to get

---

13. There was considerable controversy as to the possibility of seeing a face clearly enough for recognition by the light of a gun-flash, and the result seems to be that, though generally such a recognition would be unlikely, it might in some circumstances be possible. Here the difficulty of recognizing Vivian would have been lessened since the face was well known to Mason – and was probably that which he was expecting to see.
14. It was in this yard that the torch was found.
15. There was barbed wire on this wall, and it was probably here that Mason cut his hand. Whilst on this wall he heard someone following behind whom he thought was Vivian.

into the garden of No. 15. It was here that the dog barked, and he asked and obtained permission to pass through the house. The importance of this account of his route will be discussed later, but it may be said that if his description was correct, it almost necessarily follows that there was some second person concerned in the crime.

Crossing Acre Lane, Mason passed along Trinity Square and found a tramcar going to Victoria. He had no money but persuaded the conductor to let him remain by promising to send on the fare, and the conductor wrote his own name and address on a piece of paper so that Mason could do so. This paper, Mason declared, he subsequently destroyed on Vivian's advice.

Arriving at Charlwood Street, he found Vivian already there, and the latter described what had happened. He had found his "straight-up" taxi, had promised the driver "Jackie" £1 and a further £5 if he brought off a job, and had driven to Acre Lane. But on the way he had told the driver that he would have to wait for his money, and this had started a quarrel, the driver saying that Vivian must pay what was on the clock or he would drive to the police station. Vivian had then tried to get out, and when the driver had caught him by the coat had shot him in order to get free.

Vivian's account of his own escape was that he had managed to climb over walls to a street, had mingled with the crowd there, and had then come home via the Kennington Road. Before Mason's arrival, he had cleaned up his clothes with the towel, which Mason stated was in a filthy condition. And at the end of the story he had made a pathetic appeal to Mason, and Mason had promised that he would never give him away.

These then are the two stories between which the jury had to choose – for, though there was outside evidence connecting Mason with the crime, unless the jury believed that Vivian's story was in substance true, they would hardly have convicted Mason. For there was deadly evidence against Vivian himself in the articles found round the scene of the crime, and in fact, if not in law, the onus was on him to satisfy the jury that he was not responsible for their presence there.

Mason cut a poor figure in the box. On some points he was clearly lying, and lying clumsily at that. The walk from Victoria to Webber Row and on to Bay Tree Road could never have

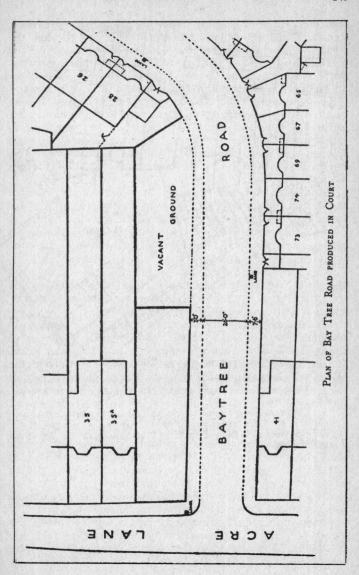

PLAN OF BAY TREE ROAD PRODUCED IN COURT

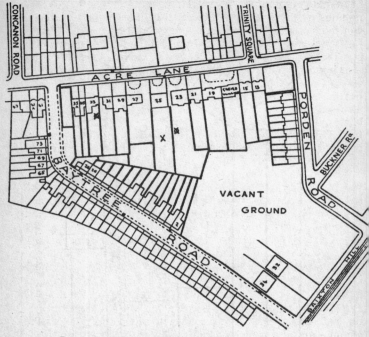

PLAN SHOWING POSITION OF ACRE LANE AND BAY TREE ROAD

The cross in the garden of No. 25 marks where the glove was found.

The spots indicated in the gardens of Nos. 23 and 33 mark the positions of the footprints.

The line across the garden of No. 27 (not in the original plan) was inserted to show the correct position of the back wall of this garden, the ground between such wall and Bay Tree Road forming, in fact, part of the garden of No. 25.

been done in the time – it would have required another twenty
minutes at the least. And there are other points where he
contradicts himself hopelessly, e.g. at one time he says
(agreeing with Vivian) that he spent Monday afternoon with
a girl called "Fluffie" at the Palais de Danse at Hammersmith
– at another time he declares that he and Vivian passed the
whole afternoon prospecting near the Crystal Palace[16].
Furthermore, his explanations of his early statements when
arrested were unconvincing. But worst of all, his story had not
been told till the last minute, when he entered the box at the
Old Bailey, and when he had heard, and had ample time to
consider, the whole of the evidence that had been brought
against him.

Vivian, on the other hand, was consistent and his evidence
was in no way seriously shaken. His story was, of course, the
easier to tell, for his own part in it was a purely passive and
negative one – he had been seedy and in bed, and had not
stirred out of the house on the Wednesday evening – the
class of story which, in the absence of external contradictory
evidence, is absolutely unassailable by any cross-examination.
And yet, perfect though his account may be in its details, there
is that in it which seems to hit you in the face – to strain your
powers of belief up to and beyond their breaking-point.

For Vivian's story centres round a cold-blooded murder,
done deliberately for the purpose of rifling the body of the
victim – and the setting of the tragedy is wholly wrong.

A taxi-driver is not usually a Crœsus – the only object in
choosing him for a victim is that, from his mobility, you can
get him where you want him. Clapham Common at midnight
– where Steinie Morrison lured a much less mobile prey, an old
gentleman who practically never left the eating-house where he
spent his days – or Wormwood Scrubs – where there might be
a chance both to kill your man and go through his pockets,
which would be the sole object of the crime. But Bay Tree
Road – at a point in full view of Acre Lane – surrounded by
houses from each of which witnesses might emerge at the
sound of the first shot – at an hour when the world was still

---

16. It should be noted, in fairness to Mason, that for some reason this discrepancy
     was never put to him in cross-examination.

wide awake: is it conceivable that any man on earth would have chosen such a spot for such a purpose?

The only explanation that seems possible is that the murder *had* to be done there because some sudden crisis had arisen – such as a threat by the driver to call in the aid of the police – a very awkward matter for a man with the record of either Mason or Vivian if he happened to be carrying a jemmy and a revolver[17].

The only corroboration for Mason's story was that of Mrs Nunn, who stated that she remembered his calling on the evening of the Wednesday. She had not actually seen him herself, as her daughter had opened the door, but she had recognized his voice[18].

Vivian's story was to some extent corroborated by Hettie Colquhon, who spoke of his having complained of illness on Tuesday afternoon, and also as to having seen Mason with the gold-headed stick in his hand just before he left on the Wednesday evening, though she did not actually see him take it out of the room.

There was, of course, other evidence telling heavily against Mason – that he was undoubtedly present when the murder was committed, and that his trousers were bloodstained, whereas there was no trace of blood on Vivian's clothes. The evidential effect of these bloodstains must not, however, be exaggerated, since Mason had cut his left hand badly and had attempted to brush his clothes with this hand, which might quite possibly have accounted for these stains[19].

---

17. It may be said that this presupposes that Dickey was in fact a "straight-up" taximan, but this is by no means a necessary inference. The fare may have been mistaken in his man – the entrance to the Trocadero is not the most convenient place for discussing a delicate arrangement of the type suggested – and the trouble may have arisen from the driver becoming suspicious and threatening to go to the police station.

18. If this evidence is accepted as true, it is important, since if Mason had been the man who hired the cab, he could not have passed Webber Row on his way from Piccadilly to Bay Tree Road, or the taxi-meter would have registered more than five shillings and threepence, as the distance would have been nearly six miles. In 1923 the taxi fare was still one shilling a mile. This point does not seem to have been presented to the jury.

19. In fact, the worst of the stains were inside his left-hand trouser pocket – and these must have come from his own wound – as must the blood on his hat. Dr Webster, the expert witness for the Crown, was not prepared to say that the other bloodstains could not have been so produced, but was of opinion that the deceased man must have bled freely, and that the stains on Mason's clothing

There had been statements too, made by Mason himself, which told heavily against him. At the time of his arrest he knew that Vivian had been taken, for he had called at Charlwood Street that afternoon, and though the constables who requested him to come to the police station said nothing as to their reason for wanting him, he could have had no doubt as to what that reason was – though he may have believed, as he declared in the box, that he was wanted on Vivian's account rather than on his own. At any rate, he made a rambling statement about Vivian and himself having been at Norbury on Tuesday night, where he had cut his hand going over garden walls, and then added that on Wednesday Vivian had been ill, and that he had gone out alone and taken Vivian's stick. Mason declared that he had said that it was a brown malacca stick (i.e. not the one found), but the police officer denied that he had mentioned this.

There was one other piece of evidence which both sides called in aid. Shortly before the trial, the prisoner's solicitor, Mr Blinkhorn, acting on information supplied by Mason, had gone to Charlwood Street, accompanied by Detective-Sergeant Harris, and had there found on the top of the lavatory cistern fifteen cartridges similar to those found in the revolver. The Defence used this as corroboration of Mason's story that Vivian had said he had put the revolver and cartridges there when Mason objected to his going armed. Vivian, on the other hand, suggested that it was a case of "those that hide can find", and that Mason had himself put the cartridges there after the murder.

---

were consistent with what he would expect from the probable position of the two men in the struggle. In the closing speech for the Crown, a good deal of stress was laid on the fact that there were no signs of bloodstains on Vivian's clothing and that when he was arrested no other suit was found than that which he was wearing. But it must be remembered that he was not arrested till the Saturday, and that there would therefore have been ample time to dispose of any incriminating evidence.

It might well have been possible to remove the uncertainty as to the origin of these stains. If tests had been applied to the bloodstains on Dickey's clothes and on those of Mason, and the blood had been shown to be of different types, the stains on Mason's clothing would have ceased to have any evidential value against him – whilst if they were of the same class the evidence would have been immensely strengthened, unless the prisoner had shown that his own blood was also of this class.

With all this self-made evidence against the prisoner, and Vivian's testimony absolutely unshaken, there could be but one result. The judge, in summing-up, impressed on the jury that it was for them and not for him to decide as to the truth of Mason's story, but he pointed out its inconsistencies, and commented most unfavourably on the prisoner's complete silence in the earlier proceedings and the concealment of his line of defence till the last possible moment. The jury, after an absence of only seventeen minutes, returned a verdict of Guilty.

Mason, being called on according to custom to state whether there was any reason why sentence of death should not be passed, admitted that he had had a fair trial, and that on the evidence he had expected no other result, but begged that the police would make further investigations which might corroborate his own story.

No doubt the trial was a fair one, but I think that anyone reading the report will feel that the case for the Crown was not prepared with that care which we generally associate with Scotland Yard. There were errors of the most obvious kind in certain parts of the evidence – omissions, actual or apparent, to collect and present to the Court evidence that lay before the eyes of the police, and which, if there were any substratum of truth in the prisoner's story, might have helped him materially.

The first criticism must be directed to the inaccuracies in the plans of Bay Tree Road and Acre Lane. These were apparently prepared from an Ordnance map, with some assistance from a surveyor as to Bay Tree Road, built since the time of the map, but without sufficient checking, especially as regards Acre Lane. This led to open spaces being shown at the sides of Nos. 23, 27 and 31 Acre Lane through which escape from the gardens to the road would have been easy had they existed, but which in fact were blocked by garages built since the date of the map. There was also an inaccuracy as to the gardens of Nos. 25 and 27 Acre Lane, and certain gates between gardens were not shown.

The next point is the lack of care in tracing the flight of the criminal. The position, as known to the police on the Thursday morning, was that a murder had been committed in Bay Tree Road, that there was no reason to think that the perpetrator had escaped on the north side, and that a man had been allowed to pass through No. 13 Acre Lane – a man who might or might not be identified.

Starting from No. 28 Bay Tree Road, the first investigations were made on a piece of vacant land at the back, accessible through a wicket gate. Broken trellis-work was found on the fence between this land and the garden of No. 33 Acre Lane, and the search was continued through the gardens leading from No. 33 to No. 13. But the evidence obtained was so vague as to be valueless. Footprints were found in some of the gardens, notably those of Nos. 23 and 33 – but footprints in a garden are not in themselves proof of a criminal visitation. The important question was *whose* footprints, and it would seem a necessary and obvious precaution to take casts of those which were plainest – necessary and obvious from the knowledge then possessed by the police, quite apart from the questions which actually arose at the trial.

For the police were not justified in relying on the chance that the man who had escaped through No. 13 would, if arrested, be identified by its occupants. Experience has shown that the identification of a man seen only on one occasion is often a matter of the greatest uncertainty, and that such an identification should never be relied on unless supported by other evidence – and a most valuable form of such evidence would have been the identity of the footprints of the suspected man with those found along the route from No. 28 Bay Tree Road to No. 13 Acre Lane.

As events turned out, such evidence was not needed for this particular purpose, since Mason admitted that it was he who had passed through the house, but it would have been of the greatest value for testing the truth of his statement that Vivian had been in Bay Tree Road, and had also escaped through No. 28.

Mason was sufficiently definite as to his own route, viz. along the wall at the back of Bay Tree Road and down from the back wall of the garden of No. 23 Acre Lane, i.e. the wall nearest Bay Tree Road, through that garden to the wall of No. 21, and then eastward through the other gardens to No. 15. The traces found by the police indicated a route from Bay Tree Road into the garden of No. 33 Acre Lane, and thence over various walls including the western side wall of the garden of No. 23. If, then, Mason's story were true, the footprints on this latter track were not made by him. Mere measurement would probably not have decided this question, since the boots Mason was wearing had belonged to Vivian. But this pair had been repaired the day before, and would have presumably given a print clearly distinguishable from those worn by Vivian[20].

If the prints in No. 33 were Mason's, his story of the twofold flight was clearly fabricated, but had they coincided with Vivian's they would have proved much more than the mere presence of a second person. For in the garden of No. 25 was found a left-hand glove which was the fellow to that dropped in the struggle with Dickey, a struggle in which (as independent evidence showed) only one man took part. If, then, there were two fugitives, the man who carried the gloves was the man who shot Dickey, and his route had been that which passed through the garden of No. 25.

There are other criticisms on this search. There seems to have been little or no examination of the wall behind Bay Tree Road – which might have disclosed marks confirming Mason's account, if that were true. And the searcher overlooked much that was obvious, e.g. the glove in the garden of No. 25, and did not even notice that the open spaces shown on the plan as existing between certain houses in Acre Lane, were no longer open[21].

It may be objected that the police could not anticipate the line the case would take, since Mason did not disclose his defence till the last moment. But this is no answer, for the time for making these investigations was long before that at which any such disclosure could have been made.

Another curious feature is the absence of any fingerprint evidence, particularly in view of the fact that the criminal, although he had gloves, was certainly not wearing them, or they would not have been dropped as they were. We may

20. No evidence was given of the nature of the repairs, but as the charge was 9s. 6d. it may be assumed that they included soleing and heeling.
21. There would have been no difficulty in the second hypothetical fugitive escaping unnoticed as from the back walls of Nos. 13–19 Acre Lane he could reach the vacant ground and make his way to Porden Road. In fact, if Mason, when on the wall of the garden of No. 15 Acre Lane, had jumped to the right instead of the left, he would have landed in this vacant land, and have in all probability escaped without being seen by anyone.

presume, I suppose, that the revolver and stick, and the taxi-cab itself, were tested with negative results – but was the search extended to the cartridge cases in the revolver, some of which, especially the undischarged one, might have given a print that would have been worth more than all the oral evidence? Some of the fifteen cartridges found at Charlwood Street might also have told an unshakable story as to who in fact was their owner.

It is rather surprising, too, that more witnesses were not found, or called, who could speak as to the actual circumstances of the crime. There was one such possible witness: Captain Carter, who, according to a newspaper account, saw something of the struggle from his window and heard all the shots, and therefore could at least have thrown light on the duration of the fight[22]. And such additional evidence might have been useful, for the crime is not an easy one to reconstruct. From the fact that the bloodstained glove, the jemmy and one of the driver's gauntlets were found twenty-five yards down the road towards Acre Lane, part of the fight must have occurred there. Possibly the struggle started by the cab and continued down the road to the point where the jemmy was found – clearly some of the wounds must have been inflicted at or before this point from the fact that the glove was bloodstained.

But Miss Findlay describes the fight as she saw it as taking place close to the cab, which would mean that the combatants had returned on their path. It must be remembered, however, that the light was very bad, and the figures mere silhouettes, so she may possibly have misjudged how far down the road the men were – and this suggestion is supported by the revolver being found by a hoarding which stopped some ten yards short of the place where the cab was standing. Unfortunately the exact point where it was found was not marked, nor does there seem to have been any attempt to trace the four bullets fired besides the two that were actually found in the body.

A possible alternative is that the fare ran off towards Acre Lane, but seeing the driver in pursuit, turned and fired, and

22. Presumably this Captain Carter was identical with the Mr Carter who, in conjunction with Sergeant Dykes, examined the taxi-meter. It was also alleged that he heard Dickey call out "Keep back, they are armed". Mason asked leave of the Court of Criminal Appeal to call him as a witness.

that Dickey then closed with him at the spot where the jemmy, etc. were dropped, probably after receiving one or more wounds.

The prisoner's story was a weak one – I have already pointed out its inconsistencies. But what told against him more than these inconsistencies was the fact that the story had not been put forward till the last moment, and here I think that the Prosecution – and, if I may venture to say so, the Court – failed to appreciate or sympathize with the real difficulties of a prisoner in Mason's position.

It may be accepted as a general rule that a defence should be put forward as soon as possible, and failure to do so leads to criticism under two heads. Firstly, it may be alleged that owing to the lateness of its disclosure the Prosecution have had no means of testing the truth of the defence, and secondly, it will probably be said that that defence is a mere fabrication, built up after the evidence for the Prosecution had all been disclosed, and so as to avail itself of any loopholes in that evidence.

The weight of the criticism under the first head depends largely on the line of the defence. If this is in the nature of an alibi, the objection of a late disclosure is very formidable, since an alibi may be met by positive evidence to show that the prisoner was in fact not where he claims to have been. The same applies if the prisoner seeks to lay the crime on some person not present in court, but who might have been found and called as a witness had due notice been given. But if the actual evidence in the present case is examined, it does not appear that the Prosecution was substantially handicapped by the absence of any earlier statement by the prisoner, since so far as Mason's positive defence was concerned, the fight resolved itself into a duel between Vivian and himself, and it is difficult to see what corroboration for his story the latter could have obtained, apart from that which was in fact given by Hettie Colquhon.

The suggestion that the murdered man was an accomplice of criminals may, indeed, have been a surprise to the Prosecution, but this suggestion was in fact withdrawn by the Defence[23].

---

23. I say may have been, because certain of the press reports on the days immediately following the murder seem to show that there had then been a rumour – though

The mere fact that the defence is not set up till after the evidence for the Prosecution has been given counts for little in itself, since that is the normal time for a defence to be disclosed, whether this be done at the Police Court or elsewhere. In many cases, it is true, there are questions put in cross-examination of the witnesses for the Prosecution which indicate the nature of the defence, but on the other hand it is quite common, even when the prisoner has legal assistance, for the cross-examination to be reserved until the case for the Prosecution has been fully developed.

However, the counsel for the Crown put forward a much more formidable line of criticism, which may be paraphrased as follows. "If the prisoner's story were true, can you believe that any man would have behaved as he has, have sat silent throughout the Police Court proceedings, throughout the hearing before the Coroner, and never have attempted, by statement or question, to show what wicked and deliberate perjury was being committed?"

To assess the value of this criticism, it is necessary to assume that there was some substantial truth in Mason's story, say to the extent that, though present in Bay Tree Road for the purpose of joining Vivian in the commission of a felony, he had no actual hand in the murder, nor had he known that murder was contemplated. Is it then compatible with normal human nature that he should preserve such silence?

Perhaps normal human nature is too high a standard to take. Mason was an ignorant man, a frightened man, and a man with anything but a clear conscience, and full allowance must be made for each of these factors in judging of his conduct.

There are endless proverbs and wise sayings on the beautiful maxim that if you are innocent, you need never fear to tell the truth. Innocent, yes – but innocent of what? Innocent of the precise charge brought against you, or innocent of all that would bring you within the clutches of the law?

---

undoubtedly an unfounded one – that Dickey had been driving burglars up and down Bay Tree Road and hooting as a signal to an accomplice.

The absence of "Jerry" who, Mason stated, met Vivian and himself at Victoria on the Wednesday evening, told against and not for the prisoner. But the name of this man had in fact been given to the police before the trial by the prisoner's solicitor, with a request that they should if possible find him, and the police had failed to trace him.

The maxim above referred to is one on which any sane being would act if his defence were that at the time he was supposed to be committing a loathsome crime he was in fact engaged at a Church Congress, at a meeting of the Independent Order of Rechabites, or in sitting happily at home with his wife and family. But when the truth involves a confession of a felonious purpose which, with his past personal record, would probably involve a sentence of penal servitude – a sentence which would be none the lighter for that felonious purpose having led to a murder, however innocent he himself might be of its perpetration – then human nature may well be capable of doubting whether silence may not be the safer course.

So far we have been considering the case of a man who knows himself to be innocent of the charge brought against him. But did Mason know that he was innocent – that is, innocent in the sight of the Law?

Mason had probably a criminal's hazy knowledge of Criminal Law – and there is no branch of that law in which the legal balance is more delicately poised than that which deals with the position of the man whose accomplice in a crime commits murder. Mr Justice Rigby Swift, in summing up the case to the jury, explained the matter with great clearness. If the murder be committed in furtherance of the common purpose, both are responsible, but if committed by one for his own ends, e.g. to further his own individual escape, or from private spite, then the actual murderer alone is guilty. And, having so defined the law, he told the jury that if Mason's story were true, he could not be held guilty as an accomplice in Vivian's crime.

This, no doubt, is the Law – but how much of it did Mason know? He was certainly aware that in some cases an accomplice may be held responsible, since he stated in the box that he had told Vivian that if he carried a revolver he would not go with him. But the finer points were certainly *terra incognita* to him and he would be continually obsessed with the dread that, if he made any statement, he might be merely putting his own neck in the noose.

The dominating feature of Mason's position was his utter loneliness. He was in prison, surrounded by persons who to him were enemies, to whom he could make no statement, of whom he could ask no question, without the danger of that statement or question being used against him. Even if he saw a friend, it was in the presence of a prison officer, and anything he said to such friend might be reported and used at his trial.

There is one exception, and one exception only, which the Law makes to the stern rule that all that a prisoner says may be used against him, viz. that he may speak freely and in private to his legal adviser and that any statement made to such adviser is privileged. But Mason had no legal adviser, nor any means of getting one, and so had to make his decisions alone and unaided. In such a case, is it really a cause for hostile comment that those decisions were not the wisest, or that an ignorant prisoner, utterly unable to judge of the probable effect of any step he might make, took refuge in terrified silence?

How anxious Mason was to obtain such advice was shown at the close of the Police Court proceedings. His one question to the magistrate was, could he have a legal adviser, and the magistrate was compelled to answer that the law did not permit him to certify for legal aid unless a prisoner had made a statement. Mason then entered the box to make such a statement, but the magistrate – judging, and probably judging rightly, that his only object in so doing was to qualify for legal aid – advised him to remain silent, and told him that the judge at the Old Bailey would assign him Counsel who could advise him as to his best course.[24]

Some five weeks elapsed between Mason's committal and his trial, and during this time funds were raised for his defence, which was undertaken by Mr Blinkhorn. Then Mason could at last speak freely, but by this time he had probably worked himself into a state when he could gain little advantage from the privilege.

It may, however, be said that, even if Mason feared to make a statement, it was not compatible with innocence that he should hear Vivian's testimony and ask no questions of him. But probably the same considerations tied his tongue here. It is not easy to cross-examine with effect whilst the lines of

---

24. This advice of the magistrate was unfavourably criticized at the trial, but personally I think it was fully justified. It was probably clear to the magistrate from the prisoner's previous silence that his proposed statement might tell heavily against him, and be of such a nature that no solicitor or counsel would allow him to put it forward, unless he had been fully warned of the danger.

defence are still unsettled, and during the earlier proceedings Mason was probably hesitating whether to tell a story such as he gave at the Old Bailey, or to rely on a denial of all knowledge of the murder either before or after its commission. The difficulties, too, are greatly increased when a prisoner has to conduct his own defence. An advocate can put questions freely, and none may ask his reasons, but if Mason had put any question betraying a knowledge of what happened at Bay Tree Road, he would have been liable, when he went into the box, to have questions put to him as to the source of that knowledge – questions which might have been fatal had his defence then been that he was not present at the scene of the murder. Probably, too, he was dreadfully aware of the pitfalls attending any cross-examination. He was a man with several convictions, and he knew that, if you put certain questions to a witness for the Prosecution, the police were justified in bringing out your own bad record – though he probably had but the haziest idea of what the dangerous questions were. And so here too he maintained silence.

Mason may have been innocent or guilty – that is a question which may never be solved, and (apart from the consequences to the wretched man himself) a question of minor importance. Under the best of human systems, miscarriages must occasionally occur – what is of importance is that the system itself should be such that the prisoner has every facility for putting forward his defence in the best possible manner.

Many other criticisms were made of Mason's evidence, some of which seem to have had little substance – notably that as to his story of the tram ride back from Brixton, when he could not pay his fare and the conductor wrote down for him his own address, so that Mason could forward this fare. The suggestion made was that, had this been true, Mason would have kept the paper, or would have asked the police to find the man so that he could corroborate his story.

Why on earth should Mason keep such a paper? On the Wednesday night, his one desire would be to destroy everything that connected him with Bay Tree Road. If he were arrested, and denied (as in fact he did at first) that he had been near Brixton that night, the police finding this paper would certainly have made inquiries of the man named on it, who would at once have identified the prisoner as a man who had travelled from Brixton shortly after the time of the murder. And what good would it have done to find the conductor and call him at the trial? – whether Mason walked or rode home from Brixton would not have afforded one iota of evidence as to whether Vivian's story or his own were the true one.

Mason duly lodged an application for leave to appeal, which was heard by a Court at the head of which was Mr Justice Darling, the others being Shearman and Branson, JJ. There was no hope of success on the grounds either of misdirection or of the verdict being against the weight of evidence, and the chief object was to obtain leave to introduce fresh evidence.

At the hearing, certain letters were produced which Mason had written in prison to a Miss Stewart and which it was claimed showed clearly that Mason had declared that Vivian was the murderer as early as 7 June. The Court read the letters, but failed to find any definite statement in them to this effect. In any case, such evidence would have been of very minor importance.

Mason also applied for leave to call a Mr and Mrs Haddock, who were alleged to have seen Mason walking away with another man, but as the proposed proof of Mrs Haddock entirely contradicted Mason's story of his escape, leave was refused. Another suggested witness was Captain Carter, to whom reference has already been made. A request was also made that the hearing might be delayed so that a statement might be obtained from a Captain Hughes, supposed to be in Brussels, who was alleged to have seen Mason and Vivian together on the night of the murder, but the Court seemed to regard this witness as a somewhat mythical character and declined to postpone the hearing. By the dismissal of the application for leave to appeal, Mason's last legal resort was exhausted, and his execution was fixed for 15 August.

Mason had been tried according to Law, and convicted by a jury of his fellow countrymen, and the Court of Criminal Appeal had found that there was no legal reason for interfering with that conviction. Yet there must have been some amongst those who administer the Law in whose minds a doubt still persisted as to whether the whole truth had become known, for on 10 August the Home Secretary, Mr Bridgeman, granted a reprieve, and commuted the sentence of death into one of penal servitude for life.

The reason for this decision will probably never be known with certainty, since it was not customary for the Home Secretary to give the grounds on which he advised the sovereign to exercise the Royal Prerogative of mercy. But certain inferences can be drawn from the facts of the case[25].

There was no question here of any mental infirmity of the prisoner which, though not amounting to legal insanity, might justify a claim that morally his act should not be judged by ordinary standards. Nor could there be any suggestion of extenuating circumstances – a more cold-blooded and unjustifiable murder was never committed if the story told for the Prosecution were true.

What possibility remains but that something had become known exterior to the evidence given at the trial, something which suggested that there yet remained some doubt as to Mason's guilt - or the degree of that guilt – a doubt sufficient to sway the balance against the irrevocable step of taking another life? Maybe there were rumblings in that mysterious underworld whence come so many of the clues that place the criminal in the dock – hints of facts which had not come to light – hints that would never be supported by sworn evidence but must be assessed by the standards of the CID – things intangible to the Law, and that could never be used to set aside the findings arrived at by the process of that Law, yet sufficient to influence the exercise of the prerogative of mercy.

In February of the ensuing year, there was a further investigation by Scotland Yard, prompted by a statement which Mason had made to another prisoner in Dartmoor that there were two other men with him on the night of 6 May, one of whom was the murderer of Dickey. Apparently this investigation produced no result, for Mason remained in prison – first at Dartmoor and later at Parkhurst, where, soon after his arrival, Vivian joined him.

Vivian had not long enjoyed his liberty. In the November following the trial, the police raided a house which they had

25. There was, indeed, a petition, bearing 60,000 signatures, praying for a reprieve, but this in itself was hardly likely to have affected the Home Secretary's decision – especially as the petition was only presented a few hours before the actual reprieve.

seen two men enter, one of whom was Vivian, the other being an American named Dawson. On hearing the detectives enter, Vivian rushed into Dawson's room, locking the door and leaving his companion at the mercy of the police.

There he paused long enough to deposit in Dawson's drawer the booty the police were seeking[26], and then made his escape by dropping from the window just as the police forced the door. Fate, however, was against him, for in the fall he fractured his pelvis – yet managed to climb a wall and reach his home, where he was arrested two days later. On being charged, Vivian complained that he was being continually persecuted owing to the part he had played in Mason's trial. "People have been striving to get me in consequence of false statements made against me at Mason's trial. Everybody regards me as a murderer, but God knows I am innocent. Since the trial my life has been threatened and I have been told that if I do not clear out of the country they would do me in or put me in prison."

Both Vivian and Dawson were convicted of receiving stolen property, Dawson being sentenced to eighteen months' hard labour and Vivian to four years' penal servitude, a sentence which was reduced by the Court of Appeal to twenty-one months' hard labour.

The last echo of the case in the press came in the following March, when Dawson made a sudden and violent attack on Vivian in the exercise yard at Wormwood Scrubs – a breach of prison etiquette which, whilst it invites condemnation, hardly excites surprise.

So matters stood till in 1927 Superintendent Carlin published his memoirs[27], which contain matter that, unless displaced, clearly called for a revision of the whole case.

To judge of the true effect of this new matter, it is necessary to mention an incident in the trial. On the last day of that trial, after Mason had been in the box and had been severely

---

26. The evidence as to this was given by the woman with whom Dawson was living, who was actually in the room through which Vivian escaped.

27. *Reminiscences of an Ex-Detective*, by Francis Carlin, published by Hutchinson. It may be well to mention that the Superintendent himself said that he had no doubt as to Mason's guilt – so that it cannot be suggested he was a witness prejudiced in his favour – nor did he seem to appreciate the conflict of his disclosures with the evidence given at the trial.

cross-examined as to the statements he had made when arrested, and as to their incompatability with the story he was then telling, the Jury asked if they might hear in turn what Vivian had said when detained – obviously with the object of ascertaining whether he too had made discordant statements.

A very reasonable request from a fair-minded layman's point of view – but there were legal difficulties in complying with it. Statements not made in the prisoner's presence could not be given in evidence against him, and therefore these statements could only be made public if the prisoner's counsel asked for them. To which Mr Fox Davies replied that as he had no idea what those statements might contain, he had not sought to elicit them. In the ordinary course of events, therefore, nothing would ever have become known as to the nature of Vivian's first statements to the police.

Superintendent Carlin, although he gave no evidence at the trial[28], had full charge of the investigations in the Mason case, to which he devotes a chapter in his reminiscences. He tells the story fully and dramatically, starting from the telephone call that awoke him at 2 a.m. on the Thursday morning with the news of the murder, relating the search after the owner of the stick, and detailing the directions he gave which led to the detention of Vivian, Mason and Hettie Colquhon.

During Vivian's detention at Brixton, he made two detailed statements to the superintendent, which the latter sets out, apparently in Vivian's own words. In his first statement, made on the Saturday, Vivian said, as at the trial, that Mason had written to him from Scotland asking for a revolver[29], and added that he had repeated his request when he came to London. Vivian then continued:

I met Scottie when he arrived in London, and I took him along

---

28. It would not therefore have been possible for the Defence to have obtained his account of Vivian's statements.

29. Superintendent Carlin said that he subsequently obtained this note and that it contained no reference to a revolver, but merely asked Vivian for money to enable Mason to carry out a job "when he came south". By "subsequently" the superintendent must, I suppose, have meant after the trial, since Sir Richard Muir told the Judge that the note was not in existence, and therefore claimed, and was allowed, to prove its contents by secondary evidence. But if the contents of the note were as the superintendent stated, this secondary evidence was the grossest perjury.

to the lodgings in Pimlico. We fixed it up to go out and do a housebreaking job together.

Scottie then told me he wanted a six-shooter. I asked him what for. He said, "I'm desperate, Eddie, I must get some money at once, and I'm going to get it if I have to do someone in for it."

I went along to a dealer in Kennington and bought a revolver. Then I went to an eating-house in Westminster Bridge Road, and left it there for Scottie.

Later on Mason and I went to the eating-house together and the owner of the place handed me over the revolver and I gave it to Mason.

In his evidence at the Old Bailey, Vivian gave an entirely different story, viz. that the revolver had been given by Nunn to Mason in the Waterloo Road in his absence, that he had no part in the transfer, and that he had never had the weapon in his possession. His story of the eating-house was that Mason produced the revolver there, with a matchbox full of cartridges, showed it to Vivian and loaded it, and that this was the first time that he (Vivian) had seen it.

The Superintendent also gives this further statement as made by Vivian on the same occasion.

"On the day of the murder" (at this stage, of course, Vivian merely said "on Wednesday") "I was in bed all day with stomach trouble. Hettie looked after me and got me my food."

Yet in the box Vivian swore that he was out with Mason on the Wednesday afternoon.

Vivian's second statement was made after the identification parade, and gave the story of Mason's return to Charlwood Street - substantially as at the trial. But his account of what Mason said, and of the subsequent proceedings, differs in such important respects from his evidence, that I give it in full.

"I picked up a taxi-driver, he [Mason] said. I told him to drive to a quiet place in Brixton. When we got to Bay Tree Road I got out, and then I made a dive for him to get what money he had on him.

He put up a big fight and I felt he was going to get the better of me. So I pulled out the shooter and fired.

That didn't stop him, although I think I hit him. He struggled again with me and I fired again and a third time. That put him out and I got a couple of quid off him.

And I've gone and dropped your stick and gloves at the place, he told me.

That frightened me, and I said something to him about the cops finding out that it was my stick and that they would try to get me for the murder.

He tried to laugh me out of that and said that the taxi-driver was dead. 'That's a good job, anyway, for he can't give any description,' he remarked.

In the morning, after Scottie had walked up and down most of the night, he went out and bought a paper and read the report of the murder. I saw they had found my stick and gloves and were trying to find out who they belonged to.

Scottie kept in all that day. I gave him food and he went out in the evening. And that's as much as I know of the affair."

Let us compare this in detail with Vivian's sworn evidence. *Point one*. At Brixton on 14 May, he states that Mason had said that he had killed the driver at the third shot, and had then rifled the body and stolen two pounds.

At the Old Bailey he swears that Mason complained that seven shots had failed to kill the driver – and there is not one word as to Mason having claimed to have got any money. Can it be believed that, if Mason had really said this, Vivian would not have repeated it in the witness-box?[30]

But we are not left to speculate as to whether this was a mere omission on Vivian's part, for we know that his proof contained a distinct statement that Mason had said he had not got any money from the murdered man. At Brixton Police Court, Sir Richard Muir in his opening speech gave an account of the conversation, from which the following is an extract[31].

Mason said, "I had no money so walked all the way home." Vivian asked him, "Where did you come from?" and the prisoner said, "Brixton. If I had shot him dead *and got his money* and still had the revolver I would have gone and done another one."[32]

---

30. Moreover, Vivian swore that on the Friday Mason had to go to a friend in Soho to try to raise some money – yet he could have spent little, since he had had his meals at Charlwood Street and slept at the house of his friend Hook.

30. This was on 23 May – only nine days after Vivian had made his statement at Brixton Police Station. The extract is from *The Times* of 24 May 1923 – though, of course, the italics are my own.

32. The first story would obviously have been untenable in view of the evidence of the eye-witnesses – Miss Findlay and Mr Berkshire. In the semi-darkness they could see little – could help not at all in identifying the assailant – but they could at least speak to the timing – that the murderer, after the last shot was fired, flung down the revolver and fled straight away.

Point two. At Brixton Vivian says Mason told him on the Wednesday night that it was lucky he had killed Dickey. At the Old Bailey he swears that Mason did not know this till he saw it in the paper the next morning.

Point three. To the superintendent Vivian stated that Mason never left Charlwood Street till the Thursday evening. In his evidence he declared that Mason had gone out at nine in the morning and returned at lunch-time – and that during his absence he had discarded the bloodstained shirt.

Point four. Vivian's statement implies that he never saw Mason after the Thursday evening. But his evidence was that Mason came back to Charlwood Street on the Friday morning – and was then told in view of the search that was being made after the owner of the stick, he had better absent himself.

There is no need to elaborate further – to consider which tale is the more probable, or which might have told the more heavily against the prisoner. The simple point is that both stories could not have been true. If Vivian had in fact made the statements which Superintendent Carlin sets out, and had these been in the hands of the Defence when he gave his evidence at the trial, he could not have survived ten minutes' cross-examination, and would have left the box so discredited that the Crown would probably have hesitated to proceed with the prosecution.

I say if, because I am most reluctant to believe that these statements could have been made as set out. I have read and re-read the chapter in Superintendent Carlin's book to see if there is any loophole of escape, any possibility of reading the passages in a different light. I have made every allowance for the fact that the superintendent was not giving evidence in Court, but was writing a book – and a most entertaining book – and possibly not verifying every reference. Under such circumstances his memory might well have got confused as to details, such, for example, as the particular day on which certain events were supposed to have occurred. But there are at least two positive statements in his story which cannot be so accounted for – firstly, that Vivian had told him that he had taken the revolver and left it in the charge of a restaurant keeper, and had later reclaimed it and handed it to Mason, and secondly, Vivian's story that Mason had told him that he had got a definite sum of money, viz. £2, off Dickey's body.

There was nothing in the evidence at the trial suggesting either of these points, and no trick of memory could have evolved them.

I have tried in every way to discount the discrepancies in Superintendent Carlin's book – for the alternative is too horrible. Are we to believe that if these statements had been made by Vivian, the police could have allowed his evidence at the Old Bailey to be given without protest – could have sat silent whilst he was denying that he had ever had the fatal weapon in his hands – when the superintendent in charge of the case knew that his original statement had been that he himself had procured it and handed it to the prisoner – and this in a trial whereon hung that prisoner's life?

And yet there stand the superintendent's own words as apparent witnesses to such an unbelievable happening.

It should be noted that the points to which I have drawn attention cannot be classed as mere trivial inaccuracies on incidental matters. The two most vital points in the case for the Crown were the proof that Mason possessed a revolver, and the story of his confession – and on both these points the Crown relied wholly on Vivian's testimony.

Remember, too, that this is no case of vague rumours throwing doubts on Vivian's evidence. The account of his statements was made by a Scotland Yard officer of the highest standing, and by the only man except Vivian himself who knew what these statements really were – or could prove them in a Court of Law.

It may perhaps be allowable to consider what effect this new evidence would have had, if it had been before the Court of Criminal Appeal.

I think few lawyers would have any doubt on this point. The jury must have been very greatly influenced by Vivian's story and, if this witness were utterly discredited out of his own mouth, the Court of Criminal Appeal could hardly have done other than quash the conviction.

It is perfectly true that even if the Court find that there have been irregularities in a trial, they may still uphold the conviction if they are satisfied that the result would have been the same had these iregularities not occurred. And it is also true that in the present case there was independent evidence, which might have justified the jury in convicting Mason. But before the Court of Criminal Appeal is justified in upholding a conviction improperly obtained, they must be satisfied not merely that the verdict *might* have been the same had the trial been properly conducted, or the wrongful evidence not given, but that there can be no reasonable doubt that the jury *would* in fact have returned the same verdict[33].

And who would venture to suggest that here? It is no criterion to eliminate Vivian's evidence altogether, and ask what would have been the verdict then. You must suppose his evidence given – and then shattered by his own previous statements. How many of those who read the transcript of the trial will say that in such circumstances they would certainly have convicted the prisoner had they been on the jury?

It is perfectly true that that prisoner was himself untruthful, yet a wise judge or juryman, knowing the weakness of human nature, makes great allowances for a man who is fighting for his own life. But perjury for the prosecution, false swearing whose object is to stand a man on the drop, is a thing infinitely more sinister, and the only motive that can suggest itself to any sane mind would be one that would place the guilt of the murder elsewhere than on the prisoner[34].

But, if Vivian's story were discredited – and Mason's account admittedly impossible – where then would the truth lie? The answer to this question may never be given, but one or two possible solutions may be considered.

Firstly, Mason's story may have been very near the truth. He may have had a rendezvous in Bay Tree Road and have walked there from Victoria – though not by the route he gave. Had he gone by Vauxhall Bridge Road and South Lambeth Road, he could easily have covered the distance in the hour at his disposal.

Why, then, the tale about calling at Webber Row to see

---

33. Compare the quashing of conviction in Oscar Slater's case on the ground that the Judge in his charge had made certain remarks as to the bearing of the prisoner's general moral conduct which might have influenced the jury. In his judgment giving the reasons for quashing the conviction the Lord Justice General said, "It cannot be affirmed that any Members of the Jury were misled . . . but neither can it be affirmed that none of them were." See *The Times* of 21 July 1928.

34. I do not, of course, say that such perjury was in fact committed, nor do I either assert or deny that the statements contained in Superintendent Carlin's book were in fact made. I simply give them in the Superintendent's own words and draw attention to the bearing they would have had on the case.

Nunn? The answer must be that it was a stupid man's lie, told with the object of manufacturing corroboration for his story. And Mason was a stupid man, or in telling the story that he did he would have conjured into his pocket on that Wednesday night some hypothetical coppers, which would have enabled him to have taken a bus down Victoria Street and a tram along the Brixton Road, and so have brought his timetable within the range of possibility.

Secondly, Mason may have been in the cab together with Vivian – either from the commencement of the journey or from some other point where he had joined it after visiting Webber Row. In such case the question of guilt might well turn on the ownership of the revolver, and we are thrown back on the duel of oaths.

And there is one witness that speaks strongly to the presence of a second passenger – *the taxi-cab itself*. For both doors were found open, suggesting that each had been used as an exit[35]. And if, as Mason declared, the struggle started on the right side of the cab – that on which the driver sits – this second passenger becomes almost a necessity, for the stick was found on the pavement to the left of the cab.

Again comes the question – why then should Mason not have told the truth? And the probable answer is that he feared that to admit his presence in the cab would have involved him as an accomplice in the murder[36].

Then there is a third possibility – based on Mason's statement made during his imprisonment[37] – namely that there were three passengers on the expedition to Brixton. If this were so, it would afford the best answer to the real puzzles in this case. Why, if Mason were innocent, should he have so long maintained silence? – Why even in the last extremity, should he have refused to tell the whole truth?

But if there were a third person involved – a man whom Mason could still class as a comrade even after Eddie Vivian

35. It is hardly likely that this opening could be accidental, for the taxi-cab door was hinged at the rear, and therefore if unlatched would tend to close up rather than to open as the speed of the cab was checked.
36. Of course, he would not in fact have been held to be an accomplice if the murder arose out of some sudden quarrel between Vivian and the driver, say on the subject of the payment of the fare.
37. See page 164.

had turned against him, and whose presence must be revealed if the true story were told in detail – then the mystery disappears – for in the criminal's code the supreme commandment reads, "Thou shalt not bear witness against thy neighbour."

In attempting the analysis of the possibilities of this puzzling case, it may well be that I have been unduly favourable to the prisoner. But I have honestly tried to get inside of the mind of such a man as Mason – weak, dishonest, amoral and by his own choice the perpetual quarry of the police – to try to picture what such a man would have done when exposed to the stress of emergency, rather than to rely on the criterion of the probable action of the normal man – a criterion of whose efficacy I have ever been doubtful, since personally I have never met a man on whom I could rely to act normally in all circumstances. The jury system may be the best that is possible – and yet it is permissible to doubt whether the standard of its twelve honest burgesses is one on which reliance can invariably be placed in deducing the motives actuating a hunted and terrified criminal.

Weak – dishonest – amoral – but by no means therefore a potential murderer, for the homicidal criminal is as much in a class by himself as the man-eating tiger[38]. And, whatever his moral defects, if Mason was indeed the victim of a miscarriage of justice, he deserves our fullest sympathy, for a man who spent ten weeks awaiting the verdict of a jury in the matter of his life, followed by three weeks in the condemned cell, may be considered to have suffered a punishment little less than that of actual execution.

---

38. It should be remembered that, apart from Vivian's testimony, there was no evidence that Mason had ever been concerned in a crime of violence or had possessed a lethal weapon.

EDITOR's NOTE. Mason was released from prison in 1937. Two years later, at the start of the Second World War, he joined the Merchant Navy. He was killed in action.

The Christmas Murders contains H. M. Walbrook's account of the Steinie Morrison case (mentioned on page 151) and Arthur Conan Doyle's examination of the Oscar Slater case (mentioned on page 171).

Nemesis in Texas

Joseph Gollomb

WRITERS OF CRIME fiction, from Voltaire, Poe, Robert
Louis Stevenson and Conan Doyle down to their current
successors, have in the main chosen as their detective heroes,
not the professional policeman, but the amateur – the scientist,
the cultured dilettante, the shrewd old lawyer, the newspaper
reporter. Whatever the reason for this preference, I want to
note here only that in real life an amateur detective would be
labouring under the same handicap against the professional as
the amateur in any other field of endeavour; broadly speaking,
the police are no more stupid than any other class of workers
and they do specialize in hunting criminals.

But when in a crime story it is a newspaper reporter who
beats the police to the solution of a mystery, fiction becomes
most plausible in the choice of amateur detective. For, by his
very calling, the newspaper reporter is daily assigned to follow
a clue to some fuller story as yet unknown to the public; often
it is actually a murder mystery or some other unsolved crime.
At such times the reporter and his editors begin with all that
the police can tell them, and in addition bring to the quest
broader background and more versatile minds. At least this is
what happened in the Payne mystery in Amarillo, Texas. And
it is a story which, if seen on the moving picture screen, would
be accepted by the mass of the uncritical as a good "movie"
and rejected by the sophisticated as untrue to life, too extreme
in both subtlety and violence of psychology and of action.

Amarillo was then a railroad centre in the Panhandle of
Texas, a town of nearly sixteen thousand inhabitants, with two
newspapers, several hotels and ample police organization; a
community that had outgrown the "wild west" instability of
life which characterized the history of the Panhandle.

Arthur D. Payne, who claimed to be a direct descendant of

Arthur D. Payne

the man who wrote "Home, Sweet Home", was one of Amarillo's leading lawyers. On the morning of 27 June 1930, he was standing on the porch of his semi-suburban, brick-and-stucco home, watching his wife, his ten-year-old daughter, Bobbie Jean, and his son, Arthur D., Junior, a boy of nine, as they were preparing to drive off in the family automobile. It was to be a shopping trip in a direction away from Payne's office, so he was not going with them. As usual he preferred to walk to his office. At the last moment Bobbie Jean decided that she wanted to walk with her father and climbed out of the car; she would meet her mother later, it was arranged, after seeing her father to his office.

The parting made one of those commonplace domestic scenes that breathe of inner peace and health. Mrs Payne at the wheel and the boy, as they drove off, turned and waved to the father and the little girl; Payne and his daughter waved back and, when the car was out of sight, left too.

At the door to his office, Payne kissed Bobbie Jean and the two parted. Ten minutes later he was in the midst of dictating to his stenographer.

His telephone rang. A man's voice came over the wire, a stranger's.

"I'm terribly sorry, Mr Payne," he was saying, "but I have bad news for you. Your automobile blew up on my beat – I'm Patrolman Brown – and I'm afraid your wife is dead. Your son, though, is still alive. You'd better come quick!" He told where.

The stenographer cried out: "Why, Mr Payne, what's happened!"

For the man had dropped the receiver with a cry, and was running out of the office without hat or coat; he was gone before she could get an answer.

About half a mile from the Payne's home, a crowd was agonized over a shocking sight. Tangled in the ruins of a car that had been literally blown apart was the body of a woman. With her was a young boy, also badly torn, still breathing between cries of pain. The woman was not only dead but unrecognizable. It was the boy who had told who they were.

When Payne arrived on the scene he grew hysterical at what he saw. It was fully a quarter of an hour before Patrolman Brown and two doctors, who had been summoned, got him at all quiet.

"Who saw it?" he demanded. "How did it happen?"

No one knew exactly what had happened, only that the car was going along at a moderate rate and had struck no obstacle at the moment when, without warning, an explosion blew it to pieces.

The boy was rushed off to hospital. Emergency treatment saved his life but he would remain scarred and crippled.

Payne himself was put in the care of a doctor who dosed him with bromides for several days. Then he went to the police.

He asked, "How could my automobile blow up as it did? What have you found out?"

The police official told him the findings of the investigation

The wrecked car

they were conducting. "Mr Payne, someone had placed a high explosive inside the car and a time-fuse set it off."

"In God's name, who did it?" Payne cried.

The police official shook his head; he had not the slightest clue so far.

"But rest assured, Mr Payne," he said. "we are not sleeping on the job. It's murder; a damned heartless piece of work. And we and the district attorney's office will work overtime on the job."

Payne's jaws were set and he clenched his fists.

"And there will be no sleep for me." he said, "until I face

the murderer!" Then he broke down again. "My wife! My son! Who would want to do that to them!"

The police official had known Payne and his family and could think of no one who was their enemy. Payne belonged to fraternal orders. Mrs Payne was popular with her neighbours, in her sewing circle, in her literary club and in her church society.The children too were liked by everyone.

The two newspapers in Amarillo were run and partly owned by Gene Howe, a dynamic, shrewd, crusading editor of the breed that is disappearing in this day of newspaper mergers. He took it almost as a personal affront that weeks passed after the Payne tragedy and the police made not the slightest headway in the hunt for the murderer or motive.

Through his papers, Howe offered five hundred dollars reward to spur on the hunt. In his own column in the Amarillo *Globe-News*, he wrote semi-sardonically that unless the police showed results soon, he would have himself appointed a special deputy to see what he could do with the case.

An hour after the editorial appeared, A. D. Payne entered Gene Howe's office.

"Mr Howe," he said, "I sure do appreciate your interest. Especially the reward you offer. I haven't been of much help myself. But I will add five thousand to your offer. And please call on me for anything else I can do to run down the fiend who killed my beloved wife and maimed my son."

"I will, Mr Payne." Gene Howe said.

After Payne had left the office, Gene Howe thought things over for a while. Then he got in touch by wire and long-distance telephone with the *Kansas City Star* and asked for one of its reporters, A. B. Macdonald.

Macdonald was one of those rarities on a metropolitan newspaper, a man almost sixty years old who was in full career of strenuous reporting. Not only did his own paper pick him for its most arduous assignments; newspapers from other parts of the country appealed to him to come and accomplish feats that had proved too much for local police. For nearly forty years Macdonald almost singlehanded had exposed quacks, frauds and powerfully-entrenched political machines. Above all he had made a name for himself for clearing up crime mysteries which baffled the police.

At Howe's invitation, Macdonald came to Amarillo, and

the two newspapermen conferred in the office of the *Globe News*.

"Now let's see where we stand." Macdonald said, when Howe had summed up all that he knew of the Payne mystery. "All we are sure of is that Mrs Payne was murdered. Who stands to gain by her death?"

"Well," Howe said slowly, "when the insurance company pays up, there will be $10,000 coming to her husband."

"All right, what about him as her murderer?"

"That's the line the insurance company has followed. They've held up the payment of the policy pending their investigation. But it doesn't seem to be a promising hypothesis. All the testimony of friends, neighbours and acquaintances agree that Payne and his wife made a picture of marital happiness: holding hands in public; spending their evenings together; and so on. Also Payne was heavily insured on behalf of his wife and the children. I've studied the man, and whatever else you may make me believe, you couldn't convince me that Payne killed his wife for her insurance."

"How about another woman in the case?" Macdonald asked. "Either as the murderer or as the motive for Payne to get rid of his wife?"

"I don't know of any," said Howe. "Nor do the police. And Payne is too well known in Amarillo to carry on with any woman not his wife and get away without gossip. There hasn't been any."

"Well," Macdonald persisted, "Payne might be able to hide a clandestine love affair from his family and his neighbours; but I'd like to question all the stenographers who have worked for him. So let's go up to his house and get a list of them from him."

The two newspaper men went to visit Payne. He received them cordially and seemed eager to help in every way he could. He did not resent Macdonald's frank questioning, and readily told him about the women who had been his secretaries.

"I've had several in the last year. My present one is Ocie Lee Humphries; you can find her at my office. At the time of my wife's death, Mable Bush was working for me. She lives on Pierce Street and is keeping house for her brother. She is about nineteen, a redhead, full of vitality and very attractive.

Look her up; she might help out your theory – I think I know what it is." He smiled wryly.

"Before her, Verona Thompson worked for me. She is about twenty-five years old; a rather commonplace woman, not particularly good-looking. She worked for me from August, a year ago, to December.

"Her predecessor was Vera Holcomb, who was with me only a short time, and I can't tell you where she is now. . . . Anything else you'd like to know, Mr Macdonald?"

"No thanks," Macdonald said. "Not for the present."

The reporter got to work on the list Payne had given him.

Ocie Lee Humphries could tell him nothing.

Mable Bush was as attractive as Payne had described her; but Macdonald had to admit to himself that she did not help out his theory.

The reporter then looked up Verona Thompson, the woman whom Payne had described as "rather commonplace and not particularly good-looking". Macdonald did find her rather commonplace; but decidedly she was better looking then Payne had led him to believe. She was shapely, smartly dressed, and had pretty eyes. Also she seemed nobody's fool. With renewed hope, the reporter went at her with questions.

Bluntly he asked her if she ever went out to lunch with Payne.

"Often." she replied quietly.

"Did you ever take automobile trips with him?"

"Many times. To –." She named surrounding towns in the Panhandle. Then she said, "Mr Macdonald, you are not the first to question me. Detectives have been at me and the insurance men have asked me about my relations with Mr Payne. Yes, I lunched with him and I went on trips with him. He talked only of work when we lunched; and it was only business trips that I went in his automobile. I was his stenographer. I don't see how that proves our relations were improper; or that either of us killed Mrs Payne."

Macdonald rose and towered over her. "Miss Thompson," he said sternly, "you don't know me; but any editor and the police of half a hundred cities will tell you that I'm not a novice at my game. I've been working on this case for over a week and I know more than you've told me. I know, for instance, that you've been seeing Payne since you quit working for him; that you've been off on trips with him that have nothing to do with business; and I know other things. Take my word for it, you are in deeper trouble than you dream. Now. Do you want to go behind bars and fight? Or do you want to help us? I will tell you only one thing to help you decide. Payne is under arrest for the murder of his wife!"

He knew none of these things, of course.

For some moments the girl confronted the reporter's attack. Then her eyes wavered, she covered her face with her hands and dropped into a chair. She began to tremble and to weep.

"Oh, my God, this is terrible! Do you suppose he really killed her?"

"Our only doubt," Macdonald said, "is how free of the murder *you* are."

At that she broke down completely and sobbed out her confession. She had been seeing Payne clandestinely. She loved him. He had told her that he loved her; that he wanted to marry her; that he would divorce his wife, leave his children provided for, go away with her and start life all over again.

She had been with him since his wife's death; and although he had told her he had nothing to do with the murder, he had said to her repeatedly and with vehemence, "Our lives, yours and mine, depend on your silence. If it is ever found out that we love each other and have been together, I don't know what will become of us."

She was hysterical by now. Macdonald calmed her. Later he convinced her that she had better cooperate with him and the police.

Macdonald then went to see Gene Howe, and the two consulted. Macdonald said, "It's only a gamble, of course, but let's arrest Payne."

"I'll say it's a gamble," Howe replied. "He's a shrewd lawyer and we can count on his making the most out of a false arrest. There will be heavy damages to pay if we can't make our bluff good."

"I'll tell you my scheme and you can decide if you want to take the risk," Macdonald said.

The scheme was so good but the risks were so heavy that Gene Howe felt constrained to call into conference with them the mayor of Amarillo, Ernest O. Thompson, a wealthy, spirited young businessman.

Thompson considered gravely what Macdonald had to say. Then he decided.

"I'll stand responsible for any damage suits Payne may bring," he said.

He took up the telephone and gave instructions to several police officials and the district attorney.

It was evening. Detectives were sent to arrest Payne at his home. Others were instructed to go to the lawyer's office, break in and search it.

Half an hour later, Payne was brought into the room in the city prison where Mayor Thompson, Gene Howe and Macdonald were waiting for him.

Payne was a tall, strongly built man with a wide forehead, dark eyes, full and direct in their look; his nose and mouth were straight and strong, his chin and jaws square. For the first time, the men in the room saw how deadly his eyes could look.

"Well, gentlemen," he said, "I hope you know what you are doing."

Mayor Thompson asked one of the detectives who had brought Payne, "You've searched him?"

"Yes, sir," the detectives replied. "Here is all he had in his pockets."

"Then take him down to the 'cooler'," the mayor said. "Through that room."

Mayor Thompson and the two newspapermen followed the arrested man and the detectives into the next room.

Here Payne saw Verona Thompson writing what was obviously a confession. Standing over her was the district attorney.

Payne looked more haggard than when he had arrived; but he had lost little of his self-possession. He turned to the mayor with an acid smile.

"I suppose this is where I'm expcted to break down and confess!" he said.

Mayor Thompson took out of his pocket two envelopes.

He said, "Suit yourself, Payne, about confessing. But take a look at these envelopes we found in your office."

He held them so that Payne could see. Each envelope bore an uncancelled stamp. One was addressed to the chief of police of Amarillo, the other to the sheriff. Mayor Thompson took out their contents. The two letters were identical in wording and in handwriting.

The writer described himself as a burglar. On the night before Mrs Payne's death, he had parked his automobile near a house where he was to get three sticks of dynamite for a burglary the following evening. When he came out of the house, the letter continued, he had gone to an automobile and, opening a compartment door for packages, put the dynamite sticks inside. He had gone back into the house and come out again half an hour later.

The letter went on to say that when he had got home and looked for the dynamite in his car, he had been astonished to find it had gone. He decided that he must have mistakenly stowed away the explosive in one of several other cars of the same make parked near his.

Now he knew, the letter concluded, that his mistake had caused the Payne tragedy. He was sending these letters anonymously. He didn't want to go to prison. But conscience had prompted him to write a confession.

Mayor Thompson put the letters back into their envelopes. "Payne," he said, "send me word when you are ready to talk."

Payne was taken down to what was known in the prison as the "cooler", an isolation cell walled in iron. He could not even see the guard who was pacing up and down the corridor outside his door.

Even a child could forsee what the "burglar's" letters would do to the case against Payne. He could claim, of course, that they were "planted" in his office; but it would be a hopeless effort.

During the night, Payne pondered in his cell. His mind worked keenly in search of some loophole in the case against him. The pacing of the invisible guard outside the iron door must have sounded like the tramp of approaching doom. The violence in Payne was now no longer hidden, and he expended it hysterically on the walls of his cell; but flesh and blood could do nothing against sheet-iron.

Exhausted, he went to the door and called for the guard. "I want to speak to Mayor Thompson," he said.

The Mayor came with his aides. They found Payne a changed man. His hardness seemed turned against himself, as if he were a duality, both a judge and a guilty man, a nemesis and its victim in one.

"I will confess in full," he said. "I will not spare myself and I will not ask to be spared. What I have been and what I have done can be expiated only by death. I want nothing but punishment."

The confession he wrote came to nearly 60,000 words.

His love for Verona Thompson had determined him to get rid of his wife. He began by trying to poison Mrs Payne. "But I didn't know enough about drugs to do a good job, so I abandoned the plan when a little strychnine did not cause her death."

Next he tried to asphyxiate her. One night while she was asleep, he turned on the gas. But before the room could fill sufficiently, she awoke violently ill, and her cries put an end to that attempt.

He then decided to take her out driving and kill her by sending the car over a cliff, after he had jumped out. In private he rehearsed what he would do; but the risk to himself was so great that he lost his nerve and changed his plans.

In the Payne home there was a small store-room, little more than a large closet, on the shelves of which lay a miscellany of objects. Payne loaded a shotgun and placed it so that the muzzle pointed at the door. Then he tied a string to the trigger and to the inside door-knob.

He asked his wife to get him something out of the closet. Unsuspecting, she opened the door. There was a report and Mrs Payne fell back, screaming. She was bleeding when Payne rushed over to her, pretending concern.

It was only her arm, however, that was wounded. Payne told at the time a plausible story of a loaded gun being jarred off a shelf in the store-room when his wife opened the door.

He waited a month before trying again. This time he chose once more his automobile as the instrument. He placed dynamite sticks, fuses and a lighting device inside the car. The fact that, but for accident, his two children would have shared his wife's fate, did not at the time seem to move him in the least, Payne said.

The confession was made public, and newspapers all over the world printed it.

In Amarillo the cruelty of the murder agitated even the most pacific of its citizens.

A mob gathered around the city jail and demanded that Payne be handed over to them.

The authorities had forseen this. While the mob was clamouring in front of the jail, Payne was smuggled through a back door and hurried off to a stronger jail in a neighbouring city.

When mob passion abated, under the persuasion of Mayor Thompson and a strongly reinforced armed guard about the jail, Payne was brought back.

Here he awaited trial. He refused to plead insanity or in any way mitigate his confession.

But he told a fellow prisoner, "I'm not going to the electric chair!"

The man to whom he said this thought the speech was only bravado.

The next day, however, Payne developed a sudden and surprising temper. He found fault with one of his keepers and struck him.

The punishment for such a thing, as he well knew, was solitary confinement in an isolated part of the prison.

Payne was taken down into the "cooler" where he had spent his first night in prison.

At the time of his arrest, when Payne was searched, the detectives had only gone through his pockets. Had they looked under his right trouser-leg, they would have found a small bottle of explosive fastened to his calf with adhesive tape.

Now that he was in solitary confinement, with no one to see what he was doing, he took out the bottle. Through the cork he worked a fuse.

As will be seen, he had planned for his attempt not only a definite place but also a certain day.

The date was 29 August. On that day, a clause in the insurance policy on his life would become operative. Payne could now kill himself without jeopardizing the ten thousand dollars the company had agreed to pay his children at his death.

He lay listening to the steps of the guard outside his cell. He waited until he knew that the man was at the other end of the corridor.

Then Payne put the bottle of explosive on his cot and lay

down with it. He lit a cigarette, puffed at it; touched the end of the fuse with the burning tip, and waited.

The explosion blew out the walls of the iron cell but harmed no one but Payne. The man who had once been shocking for his cruelty had carefully contrived to be the only one to die.

At his burial, a wish he had expressed was carried out, thereby giving an unintended but savage touch of irony to Payne's story. Proud to the last of his distinguished ancestor, the composer of an undying song, Payne, the murderer, had asked that "Home. Sweet Home" be played. And it was.

Killed After a Cuddle

Bernard O'Donnell

THE TWILIGHT of a dreary December evening of 1923 had faded into night, and the cold glare of electric light shone down upon the stern face of Mr Justice Avory and George William Iggulden, the prisoner in the dock, when the latter stood up to receive the last dread sentence of the law.

It had been a momentous trial in more ways than one, for the learned judge, with that unyielding respect for the letter of the law which it was his duty to administer, had laid down to the jury the legal position as regards the plea of insanity which had been put forward, and had told them frankly that, in accordance with the oath they had sworn, they had to "administer justice according to law, and not according to the view of medical men".

The crime itself had many unusual features, and it is necessary that these should be related in order that you shall have a better understanding of the unerring manner in which Mr Justice Avory guided the jury through its many intricacies.

Peering through the door of a taxicab outside Chelsea Police Station, a police officer saw, by the light of a street lamp, the dead body of a beautiful woman huddled up on the floor.

A few moments before, an agitated man with blood-stained hands had rushed into the police station, and, handing the inspector in charge a handbag dripping with blood remarked:

"Here you are. It belongs to a woman in the taxicab outside. I did it with a razor".

In the woman's throat was a deep wound, and close by was an open razor.

At the subsequent inquest a remarkable story was unfolded. The woman was something of a mystery, as, although at the house where she lodged she was known as Mrs Ethel Howard, she had also been known as Ireland. She had married a man by that name, who had divorced her; she had then lived with the co-respondent for a time; he had left her stranded and friendless; she had next lived with a man named Howard who had come into her life. This attachment also waned, and it was afterwards, when she was living in a block of mansions at Shepherd's Bush, that she made the acquaintance of Iggulden, who had inserted the following advertisement in a West London local paper:

> Lonely bachelor desires marriage with homely person (spinster or widow); advertiser is genuine and sincere, and will appreciate fully descriptive replies, with photo if possible.

Such was the advertisement that was to lure Mrs Howard, or Ireland, into a romantic association which was to end in her death on Thursday, 15 November 1923 – the day she had believed she would become a bride. A tragic and pitiful story, as she left three little children behind.

Iggulden was an unemployed butcher at the time, but he had a great gift for portrait-painting, and had been occupying his enforced leisure by painting portraits, a few of which he was able to sell. He must have been a strange fellow, for it was given in evidence at his trial that he used to curl his hair with curling-irons just like a woman, and when he stood in the dock on trial for his life, it was evident that he had taken the greatest pains, and had strained fashion to the uttermost, to present himself in the best possible light to the jury who held his life in their hands. His long wavy hair was burnished till it gleamed; his moustache was well-drilled and immaculately waxed.

When he gave himself up at the police station he was searched, and two letters which he had written before he set out from home that day were found in his possession. One was to the woman whom he had murdered, and the other was to his father; there were passages in both which threw an illuminating light on his hopeless outlook on life at the time of the crime. These were afterwards read at his trial.

At the police station he made a long statement, and it was around this statement that the defence partly built up their case for insanity, although, in the main, they depended upon the evidence of Dr Norwood East, the senior medical officer at Brixton Gaol, and Dr Hyslop, the famous mental specialist.

At length, after he had been committed for trial on the Hammersmith Coroner's warrant, both coroner and foreman of the jury declaring it to be "an utterly motiveless crime", Iggulden came before Mr Justice Avory, and at once Mr John Horridge, his counsel, applied that the jury should be sworn to try the issue of insanity, and whether the accused man was sane enough to be tried.

Dr East was called, and in reply to a question as to whether Iggulden was "in a position to follow the proceedings", replied that he was. He added, however, that he did not think that Iggulden was in a fit state to instruct counsel, as he was suffering from delusions, but would not give any information about his delusions, as he thought he would be brought in insane. In his opinion, stated the doctor, Iggulden was suffering from melancholia.

Right to the point came the first question of the judge:

"How do you know that he is suffering from delusions?" – "He told me that, about a week before the murder, he came home and remained downstairs all night because he thought detectives were after him, and in the morning he was found hiding under the table. So far as I know, there was no reason for him to suppose that detectives were after him."

"He may have had some reason you do not know of for thinking detectives were after him?" – "Yes, my Lord. He also said that people passed remarks about him, and he remained indoors months at a time because of it".

"Was there any reason for that?" – "He said he was unable to get work, and people made remarks about his blushing."

In reply to other questions, Dr East said that the prisoner had told him that he thought he was quite right in committing the crime, and would act in a similar way again.

"He thinks that wrong action perfectly right?" – "Yes".

The prisoner's maternal aunt had been in an asylum, and one cousin was an idiot, declared the doctor. Iggulden had had a desire to throw himself over Putney Bridge, and had on several occasions drunk chlorodyne.

In his opinion, the accused was insane, and unfit to plead.

Dr East was one of the most eminent doctors in the country, and had probably had more experience of insane murderers than any other man living. Yet, as Mr Justice Avory pointed out to the jury, there was an important divergence of opinion on the question of insanity between doctors and lawyers.

"In this case," the judge went on, "Dr East has stated that the accused is unfit to plead, but he has admitted that he was able to follow the proceedings of the court. If the prisoner was able to do that, and understood what the witnesses said against him, it is for the jury to judge whether he was not able to give instructions to counsel for the purpose of his defence".

Then occurred one of those utterances which indicated the unfailing observation of Mr Justice Avory.

"I have noticed", he said, "that the prisoner has taken a lively and apparently intelligent interest in every question put, and in these circumstances it is for you to decide whether you think he is fit to plead or not".

It was a remorseless, yet perfectly logical and commonsense reading of the law, and the jury found that Iggulden was fit to stand his trial.

It was then that the full story of the tragic romance was revealed in all its poignancy. Iggulden had given a false name to the woman who had replied to his advertisement. The name was Norman Hazlett, and he described himself as a portrait-painter, representing himself to be of good position in life. When the unhappy woman, tiring of her illicit partnership with men, saw the chance of becoming happily married again, she gladly gave herself to the good-looking man who paid such ardent court to her.

There is little doubt that Iggulden was very fond of the dead woman. They had arranged to be married. The woman had put up the banns at the local registry office, and on the day of the tragedy had told the landlady of the flat which she occupied that she was going out that morning to be married.

Instead, she was going to her death at the hands of her lover. For Iggulden had deceived her, knowing that he had not the means to marry her. Not long before the end, he had obtained a loan from a firm of moneylenders, posing as manager of a butcher's shop, and giving his father's name. The moneylender had telephoned the father and discovered the truth, and Iggulden had been compelled to return the loan.

But let his statement, as made to the police, tell its own lurid story of the crime. After describing how he came to meet

Ethel Howard through the advertisement, he related how he used to visit her regularly and became very devoted to her. The statement continued:

"She wanted me to marry her, and told me her husband wanted to re-marry her, also that she was afraid of him. She became very fond of me, and in fact I intended to marry her. I would have married her before now had I been in better circumstances."

The statement then moves on to the day when the end came. He went to her flat in the morning, and they went out together. They returned about one o'clock, and again went out together at three. They walked to Hammersmith, and thence took a bus to Piccadilly, where they looked round the shops. And here comes one of the most sensational parts of the statement:

"She had, during the course of our acquaintance, continually expressed the wish to die, and had said on many occasions that she was fed up with life. . . . We hired a taxicab near the Regent Palace Hotel and told the driver to go to Brompton Road. We both got into the cab, and she said, 'I would be happy to die now if the children were here now'. She repeated this two or three times.

"I was cuddling and kissing her when I seemed to lose control of myself. I took my razor from my pocket, and I cut her throat with one slash. I at once saw the seriousness of what I had done, and I told the driver to drive me to the nearest police station."

The letters found upon him give ample indication of the hopelessness which had seized him, and from their contents it would appear that he had intended to take his own life when he set out from home that day. The one written to the dead woman suggests this. It read as follows:

My Own Darling Ethel,
    You are going to have some more trouble, poor kid! I am drinking my chlorodyne now. I simply cannot face life as it is. It needs more pluck than I've got. Please, my darling, don't curse me. I shall go to hell quickly enough.
    Keep on fighting life, and you'll get the reward some day. Gee, you have had a rough life, haven't you? Never mind, I am a cad to have led you on, but I loved you so.
    Kiss darling Billy and Betty for me, and tell them daddy has gone on a long journey.

Bye-bye and God bless you.

NORMAN

The other letter, written to his father, indicates the same intention:

Dear Dad,

I am now handing in my checks by drinking a bottle of chloro-dyne. It sounds silly, doesn't it? But take it from me, Dad, it's a terrible sensation. It's called suicide, but it's something different. One finishes with an old coat when he is tired of it, or finishes up a job when he is tired of that. It is the same with life. I am tired of my life, so I am finishing it.

Very simple, isn't it? I am as sane as you are, Dad, but nobody will believe it. I have made a thorough mess of my life, and its near time I gave you a rest. But the only good turn I can do you is to roll up, so I am doing it.

I am supposed to be married next Thursday week, but, as you know, I can't. We love properly, but it is no good caring for a girl one cannot marry, is it? But that is not why I am kicking off the earth, Dad. I am absolutely weary in soul.

Your club money I used to help a dear pal, and I know you won't begrudge it. Whatever you think of me, don't think I have deliberately used your cash. I would not steal a fag paper from you without asking you for it, you know.

Don't worry your head over me, best of dads, but let me just drop out quietly. Tell people I have suffered with my heart and died in my sleep, or you'll get no insurance money. Good-bye, dear Dad. Kiss all for me.

Your weary son,

GEORGE

Say a prayer for me. Just one little favour, Dad. Will you see that none of my papers or letters are read?

In my pocket under my bolster you will find a roll of letters in brown paper. Will you post them, as they are to C.G.?

Poor kid, she loved me, didn't she? The rest you may burn, Dad. Well, I have just finished the bottle and feel rather sleepy, so will knock off now. Good-bye, Dad.

GEORGE

On the face of it, from these two letters, it would appear that suicide, and not murder, was his obsession on the day of the crime. But Mr Justice Avory elicited an important point. It was during the evidence of Dr East, who in reply to counsel for Iggulden stated that he was of the opinion that the prisoner was insane, and that at the time of the occurrence he did not know that what he was doing was wrong. That is the main essence of legal insanity. In reply to another question, he stated that he thought Iggulden knew that he was cutting the woman's throat.

And then came the question of the learned judge:

"Did he say why he taken the razor with him"?

"To shave at Mrs Howard's", was the explanation.

The fact remains that Iggulden had carried that razor about from early morning till the late afternoon when he committed the crime, and there was his own statement that under that sudden impulse he had taken the razor from his pocket and slashed the throat of his sweetheart.

But it was not around the facts of the crime itself that the battle for Iggulden's life was waged. It was around the medical evidence.

Dr East described how the prisoner said he thought he was doing the proper thing to cut the woman's throat, and that he was "doing her a service". He knew when he did it that he would be liable to punishment, the doctor agreed.

"You accepted as Gospel truth everything the prisoner said to you? Is that the foundation of your opinion"?

"I found it on the material I had", was the reply.

Then Dr Hyslop was called, and described how, during a conversation he had with Iggulden, the latter assured him that he was quite sane, and related how he had been seized with his sudden impulse to put the woman out of her misery, and *put her in a comfortable position to die*.

Dr Hyslop said that he did not think the accused could have prevented himself from committing the crime. "The idea came into his head, it became imperative, and he acted upon it. I think he was suffering from melancholia." He added that he had examined Iggulden that morning, and was of the opinion that he was of unsound mind and understanding.

Then, in reply to Mr Justice Avory, the witness stated that he thought that if Iggulden had been sane he would have tried to escape from justice, instead of giving himself up at the police station.

"Is that another way of saying that anyone who has a

conscience is insane"? queried the judge drily, and the doctor replied:

"He did not wish to escape. His great desire was to find a way out of life".

Mr Justice Avory then began his summing-up, and, with his usual clarity, simplified the legal position so far as the jury were concerned. The question for them, he stated, was "whether the prisoner was conscious that his act was one he ought not to do".

If he was, then he was not insane in law. The medical witnesses, he went on, had admitted that they had formed their opinion entirely on what the prisoner had said to them. The jury must consider whether that was a safe guide for them in the circumstances.

"The prisoner had protested against being considered insane. He knew that they were examining him in order to try to ascertain whether he was insane or not. He knew that if he were found to be insane he would thereby escape the extreme penalty of the law. Was it not almost childish to suppose that you could rely on a man's statements in such circumstances?"

Again that unanswerable logic. He dealt with the fact of the razor having been taken out that morning, the skein of difficulties in which Iggulden had involved himself by his false stories regarding his position. He invited the jury to consider the demeanour of the accused man through his trial.

Iggulden had displayed a keen interest in the evidence: had scribbled notes as the evidence was given; had followed the questions of the judge with a lively appreciation of their significance.

The jury were absent only fifteen minutes before they returned with a verdict of Guilty.

Iggulden, except for biting the ends of his moustache, was unmoved whilst sentence of death was passed upon him. Then for a moment or two he stood shifting from one foot to the other, until a warder touched him on the shoulder. Then with a bow to the judge, he passed below.

Then, and not till then, the foreman of the jury intimated that they wished to add a recommendation to mercy, and the judge ordered a warder to convey the information to the prisoner.

That recommendation evidently had the desired effect, for

after further medical inquiry into his mental condition, the Home Secretary advised the King to respite the capital sentence and order the removal of Iggulden to Broadmoor Criminal Lunatic Asylum.

A Murder in Camelot

Albert Borowitz

AT THEIR WEEKLY MEETINGS, the Leader told them about his plans. The uprising would begin when the country's economy collapsed. Atop Mount Tamalpais, the sequoia-wooded peak that dominated the Bay area, a laser-gun would be aimed towards San Francisco across the Golden Gate Bridge. The rebels were to seal off all roads leading in and out of Marin County and establish fortified headquarters in the romanesque castle-like buildings of the San Francisco Theological seminary that were perched on a hill in San Anselmo; both the Golden Gate Bridge to the south and the Richmond-San Rafael Bridge that connected Marin County with Contra Costa County to the east must be destroyed. Prisoners would be released from San Quentin Prison because the insurgents did not want to take responsibility for them; no doubt the convicts would take a cue from the Leader's example and return spontaneously to the paths of virtue[1].

When Marin was isolated from the rest of California, it would be transformed into a kingdom on the model of Camelot. What the Leader had in mind was not the sentimentalized Broadway Camelot of Lerner and Loewe that had in retrospect become a symbol of the era of President Kennedy, but the ancient British realm over which King Arthur and his forebears (or wise monarchs much like them whose names are lost to history) had actually held sway. The Leader was to serve as benevolent "Pendragon" of Imperial Marin, and his teenage followers would be elevated to knighthood.

Some of the would-be knights had their doubts about the scheme; they pointed out diplomatically that the laser-gun to

---

1. The main source of this essay is the news reports of the *Marin Independent Journal*, which provided the principal coverage of the crime and trials described herein.

be placed on "Mount Tam" had not yet been invented. True, the Leader conceded, but financing had been obtained for other weapons, including machine-guns and missiles, and stockpiling was under way on Mount Tam and in Fresno. When members of the Pendragon group went beyond expressing reservations and decided to leave the ranks of the weird conspiracy, the Leader threatened that disclosure of his military plot would mean death.

The Leader's secrets were well kept until a man's body was found floating near the Sisters Island in San Pablo Bay, the northward fist of San Francisco Bay that thrusts beyond the narrows spanned by the Richmond-San Rafael Bridge. The body, recovered on Tuesday night, 13 July 1982, by a tugboat operator for the Basalt Rock Co., was wrapped in a plastic tarpaulin and a bamboo screen, bound at the neck and ankles with television cable, rope and duct-tape, and weighted down with a small outboard motor. The dead man was thirty-six-year-old Richard A. Baldwin, the owner of a vintage-auto restoration shop, The Classic Car, on Front Street in San Rafael; the left side of his skull was fractured and he had been stabbed to the heart.

At 7 a.m. on Friday, 16 July, investigators from the police forces of San Rafael and San Anselmo and the Marin County sheriff's department arrested Mark Richards, aged twenty-nine, and two seventeen-year-old boys as they were leaving Richards's house in Sleepy Hollow in a pickup truck. Richards, a friend of Baldwin, was a home-renovation contractor, and his two companions, Crossan David Hoover and a youth named Andrew[2], were employees. The detective team had been led to the scene of the arrests by Hoover's loose talk: fellow workers had heard "Crossie" boast that, in Richards's presence, he had clubbed and stabbed Baldwin to death at the auto shop on 6 July. The police believed that the murder conspirators had taken Baldwin's house-keys from the shop and used them to burglarize his residence of several guns, a plastic trash-bag full of marijuana, and a safe. The marijuana and some guns were recovered on Friday in searches of the

2. Since Richards's second accomplice was ultimately protected as a juvenile in a decision of a California appellate court, only his first name will be used in this article.

homes of Richards and the two boys, but the safe was not yet found.

After being taken into custody, Hoover kept talking. In a ninety-minute confession, he told the police that his employer had planned the killing; the contractor had told him that his business was "hurting for money" and claimed that Baldwin owed him $3000. Hoover had agreed to the murder when Richards promised him $5000 and a car. In admitting that his offer persuaded him, the young man candidly revealed that his only regret was poor planning:

> I've been stupid. I should have gotten the cash before so I could have taken off for Brazil or someplace. . . . I didn't want to hurt the man. It was the money; all I wanted was the $5,000 and the car. Richards got my mind so psyched up that I freaked out. . . . I did it all . . . Just put me away.

At the time of the murder, Richards, Hoover and Andrew were remodelling Baldwin's home. Hoover said that Richards and he had lured their victim to the auto shop on the pretext of looking at his inventory of classic cars. When Richards scratched his head as a prearranged signal, Hoover slugged Baldwin on the head with a baseball bat and hit him three more times after he fell; he then stabbed him with a knife and a screwdriver. Afterwards, Richards and he returned to Baldwin's home, where Andrew had been standing guard, and removed the safe and other property. They then wrapped the body at the shop and used a boat Richards had just purchased to deliver it to what they vainly hoped would be a final resting place in the bay.

Mark Richards was also interviewed by the police shortly after the arrest. He denied any involvement in the murder of his good friend Baldwin and offered an account of his whereabouts on 6 July that did not ring true. The two boys arrested with him were his employees, he told Sheriff's Sergeant Richard Keaton, and then startled his questioner by adding: "The poor kids – I mean, I should take the fall for this, not them. OK? You know, like if somebody is trying to go down [take the blame] for anything."

Keaton asked, "Why should you take a fall?"

"Well, you know." answered Richards, sinking further into the morass of his own words and uncertain whether it was better to incriminate the boys or to defend them, "I understand what it must look like. OK? And all I'm saying is these are kids. You know, they don't have – they wouldn't have had anything to do with anything like this. Dick didn't owe them any money or anything like that."

After waiting patiently for the strange monologue to run its course, Keaton confronted Richards with evidence that he had used Baldwin's credit-cards and burglarized his home. Richards admitted both allegations, explaining that the car-dealer owed him money; he had used the credit-cards with Baldwin's approval in reduction of the debt. He could not plead the dead man's consent to the burglary, but apparently hoped that the detective would regard the break-in as a frustrated creditor's last resort. Still, once it was clear to him that he could not deny possession of some of the fruits of the crime, Richards backed away from his earlier "protective" attitude towards his young employees; he told Keaton that Crossie Hoover had confessed to him the murder of Baldwin.

These first statements taken from the suspects might have indicated that the killer or killers of the classic-car dealer had acted from routine theft motives. However, a police inspection of Mark Richards's house added a whole new dimension to the case. On 22 July the *Marin Independent Journal* reported the results of the search under a towering headline, "**Bizarre plot for Marin coup?**" The reporter, Erik Ingram, warned the community, better known for suburbanites relaxing in hot tubs than for corpses floating in its bay, that behind the Baldwin murder "may be a secret organization, called Pendragon, that appeared to be planning an armed takeover of Marin". Ingram reported that among the detectives' startling finds were maps, aerial photographs of Marin County, plans for a laser-gun, instructions for the construction of machine-guns, and "notebooks containing references to a new form of government"; the investigators had also taken away a number of weapons.

The suggestion that Baldwin's murder was part of a plot to overthrow the government of Marin sparked a many-sided controversy. Carl Shapiro, a San Anselmo attorney representing Richards, called the report of the Pendragon conspiracy "absurd upon absurd" and asserted that the documents found by the police were research materials for a science-fiction book Richards planned to write about a Marin of the future. Shapiro's explanation was backed by Richards's wife Caryn, who added rather vaguely that her husband's fantasy novel, entitled *Imperial Marin*, might have been published recently in Los Angeles. The staff of the *Independent Journal* could find no such listing in *Books in Print*.

The local police were also quick to discount the Pendragon plot. The head of the investigation team, Captain Richard Douglas, overwhelmed with inquiries from the media, stated authoritatively: "This is a homicide for financial gain." He regretted the "silly fantastic stories about some group taking over Marin" that might result in the trial-venue being changed from the county at added expense to taxpayers. The *Independent Journal* did its best to calm the fevers aroused by its own uncovering of the Pendragon group. In an editorial of 28 July 1982, the newspaper humorously warned against the assumption that "being a fantasy buff suggests criminal intent". The article cited an array of local fantasy activities, including the third annual "Battle of San Pablo Bay", in which "the airmen drop bombs (sacks of flour) on a Gaelic flotilla (pleasure boats) and then, afterwards, friend and foe share refreshments". In a separate news-item, the *Journal* noted the unfortunate coincidence that a San Francisco shirt-manufacturer was named Pendragon Productions and had as a consequence received numerous hostile telephone calls since the conspiracy story broke. The newspaper assured its readers that the shirt-makers were in no way connected with the crime.

In the weeks that followed, a number of witnesses came forward with stories indicating that the Pendragon group in fact existed. Crossie Hoover told investigators that one of the inducements to the murder was Richards's promise to appoint him Duke of Angel's Island. The mother of a Novato youth informed the *Independent Journal* that her son had left the group a month before because Mark Richards "was getting really weird". Another person close to Richards told the newspaper that Mark was fascinated with mediaeval history and talked about taking over all of California – a dream that did not prevent his friend from describing him as "enthusiastic and not at all sinister". The *Independent Journal* also learned of Richards's plans in 1977 to lease the San Francisco Theological Seminary building for use as a school to study the future. According to a proposed catalogue, the school, called

Futurecastle, would be an "innovative academic community dedicated to the origins of a new renaissance". The ambitious project, which was to provide a faculty including actor William Shatner and writer-producer George Lucas, came to nothing when the seminary cancelled the lease for nonpayment of rent.

In a court affidavit, another teenage employee of Richards, Pete Neal, disclosed that Hoover was not the only person Richards had solicited to murder Baldwin. Neal stated that in late May Richards had offered him a dune-buggy and $1000 as a reward for disposing of the car-dealer. Another young man told the *Independent Journal* that he had attended a Pendragon conclave some months ago but found it "too far fetched" to take seriously. He had been invited to the four-hour meeting by a friend who had reportedly been paid $500 by Richards to recruit Pendragon members.

In August 1982 a preliminary hearing of the charges against Mark Richards was held in the Marin Municipal Court. The star witness was Andrew, who had been given immunity from prosecution in return for his testimony about his participation in the murder plot. Andrew confirmed that Baldwin had been murdered so that the killers could rob his house and sell his vintage cars. The crime had been planned months in advance, and Andrew was to receive $2000 to stay at the Baldwin house while the murder was in progress. The young witness had trouble recalling times and dates, testifying that the three confederates had bought a boat a few days after the killing; the purchase was in fact made on the evening of the murder. Andrew recalled more clearly the trio's misadventures in disposing of the body. Richards, Hoover and he had put the boat in the water at the Loch Lomond Marina in San Rafael and returned to Baldwin's shop, where the body was hidden under a car. After they had brought the corpse back to the boat in a pickup truck, their troubles had begun. The boat-engine had stalled several times as they headed out into the bay, and they had been forced to drop the body closer to shore than planned. A carton of weights intended to sink the body to the bottom of the bay had broken the rope binding it to the body, so the small outboard motor had been substituted. Asked by Richards's attorney Shapiro whether he had ever considered going to the police prior to the murder with a report of Richards's plot against Baldwin, young Andrew seemed offended by the notion: "We weren't going to turn Mark in just because he was talking about killing somebody."

Judge Gary Thomas was satisfied by the evidence offered at the hearing and ordered that Richards be committed for trial.

Before the trial began, the lawyers battled over the maximum punishment that could be imposed in the event of conviction. On 9 April 1983 it was announced that the Marin district attorney's office would not seek the death penalty because of Richards's lack of a criminal record. However, the prosecution filed statutory charges that, if proved at trial, would justify life inprisonment without parole. Three of these so-called "special circumstance" allegations were sustained in a pre-trial ruling by the appellate court which found adequate ground for the district attorney's claims that the alleged crime was a murder for financial gain, in connection with a robbery, and in preparation for a burglary. Despite this adverse ruling, in December Richards was ordered released on $250,000 bail pending his trial, which had been rescheduled during the appeal for early 1984.

On 11 January the defence filed a motion seeking to prohibit use of any evidence relating to the Pendragon conspiracy. Dennis Riordan, one of the defence lawyers, argued that the alleged financial motive for the murder reflected in the special-circumstances charges filed by the prosecution had no relation to the Pendragon group. He voiced the concern that a jury of Marin residents would be prejudiced by the introduction of documents that would be claimed to reflect a bizarre plot for an armed takeover of the county.

In response, Deputy District Attorney Berberian side-stepped the question of the reality of the Pendragon plot, contending that the prosecution was entitled to show that Richards had used his dream of conquest as a means of manipulating two teenagers who were "not mental giants". Berberian further suggested that if the defendant could persuade the boys that Marin could be turned into a kingdom, he could also incite them to help murder Baldwin. A week later, Marin Superior Court Judge E. Warren McGuire ruled that the Pendragon evidence was admissible, basing his ruling on a California Supreme Court decision to the effect that Charles Manson's relationships with other members of his cult

Mark Richards entering the court

were relevant to the murders of actress Sharon Tate and others in 1969.

When the long-delayed trial at last began, Carl Shapiro acted as Mark Richard's chief counsel. In his opening statement, Shapiro charted a line of defence that was an elaboration of the tack taken by his client in the first police interview:

Richards, he argued, had participated in the attempted cover-up of Baldwin's murder but had done so only out of misguided loyalty to his teenage employees, Hoover and Andrew, who had clubbed and stabbed the victim in the course of a burglary of his home in which Richards took no part. Deputy District Attorney Berberian, in the prosecution's opening statement, claimed that it was Richards who had masterminded the killing in order to clear the way for the burglary. He told the jury that handwriting experts would testify that it was Richards, not the two teenagers, who had signed cheques and credit-card receipts in Richard Baldwin's name and had also used the dead man's name in applying for credit at a stereo store. Exercising the authority he had been given by the pre-trial ruling, Berberian announced his intention to show that Richards had formed the Pendragon group. The prosecution, he explained, did not undertake to prove that Richards was planning a takeover of Marin county, as some Pendragon members believed, but would seek to establish that the defendant had used the group to "manipulate and condition Mr Hoover to accomplish the murder".

The prosecution's evidence began with a videotape of the classic-car shop and evidence that the police had gathered there, including a blood-smeared and broken baseball-bat. The jury also heard a recording of Richards's interview with the police.

A college student who had worked for the contracting firm in the summer of 1982 testified to his surprise that in the days following the murder Richards had purchased a boat, new video equipment, and jewellery for his wife. These signs of affluence struck the witness as particularly odd since his first paycheck from Richards had been dishonoured by the bank. When the witness had noticed on the floor of the defendant's garage a safe that had been "punched open", Richards had explained that it had been given to him by a person for whom he had done remodelling work. The witness had alerted Marin detectives after another employee told him that Hoover had been boasting about killing a man and burglarizing his home.

This introductory evidence was followed by the testimony of the prosecution's "baby-faced" star witness, Andrew. According to him, Richards had first mentioned the idea of killing Baldwin on 1 July 1982. He had told Andrew and

Hoover that Baldwin owed him money, was a "Nazi" and a "faggot", and that it "would be a service to the public to get rid of such a menace". After the murder, Richards had expansively asserted that "if we made enough money, he could use some of it to buy guns for Pendragon", but Andrew was sceptical, continuing to believe that money was the motive. Richards, he testified, needed cash to save his contracting business from bankruptcy. The contractor had told his two young confederates that they might raise as much as $50,000 by selling Baldwin's property, including shop equipment and vintage cars. Andrew also described a nervous moment during the launching of the boat at the Loch Lomond yacht harbour: they had been noticed and questioned by a security guard, but had apparently satisfied him with their answers. When they returned to the marina with Baldwin's shrouded corpse, the guard questioned them again but let them pass. It was perhaps just as well for the guard that he had not looked more closely, for all three men were armed with pistols. Andrew stated that Richards had told him that Baldwin's classic-car collection could be sold through a Fresno automobile-dealer named John Carrington.

The latter, who was the next witness, testified that he had read part of Richards's science-fiction manuscript, entitled *Pendragon*, and that "it involved the separation of Marin from the rest of the country."

At this point the trial was interrupted by a startling diversion: Judge McGuire ordered special courtroom security measures after hearing the prosecution's allegation that the defendant had been seen with a gun. The judge announced that he would rule later on a motion by Deputy District Attorney Berberian that Richards's bail should be revoked and he should be returned to jail. The judge's action was based on testimony from San Rafael detective-sergeant Ted Lindquist. He had been informed that Linda Lipes of San Rafael, who was dating Richards (divorced from his wife since the murder), once felt a gun under Richards's coat and on another occasion saw a pistol in the glove-compartment of his car.

When Miss Lipes was called to testify, matters began to take a comic turn. She said that Richards had identified himself as François Ragocazy, a South American consular official, and had introduced his mother, Lois, as an aunt. Apparently fearing that she might recognize him from newspaper photographs, he had told her that a cousin, named Mark Richards, was in trouble with the law. When she asked him why he kept a gun in his car, the fictitious diplomat had told her that he needed it for "political reasons". Defence attorney Shapiro put Richards on the stand to respond to Miss Lipes's testimony. Everything she had said was true, he acknowledged, but he had not known that the gun was in the glove-compartment of the car, which he had borrowed from his father. He had quite a different explanation for the gun's presence when Berberian asked him to clarify his comment to Miss Lipes that it was there for political reasons. Richards answered: "I see this trial as political. You and Lindquist are trying to save your necks from a bad bust [arrest]." After hearing the testimony, Judge McGuire ruled that the evidence that Richards knowingly possessed a pistol was not strong enough to justify either increasing the bail or returning the defendant to prison.

The trial resumed with additional evidence regarding the operation of the Pendragon group. Mike Fuller, a former employee of Richards, stated that Willie Robles, a fellow employee, had approached him about joining Pendragon and that Richards had later warned him that he would "be eliminated" if he said anything to outsiders about the group. Robles had testified earlier that Richards paid him to recruit members. A friend of the defendant told the jury that Richards had taken him to the top of Mount Tamalpais to show him the promised land of the new Marin and to demonstrate his plan for the insurrection; Richards had said that "we could blow up the Golden Gate Bridge down there, and we could blow up the Richmond-San Rafael Bridge and destroy the Richmond oil refineries. And if we went farther north and blew up the bridge to Petaluma, Marin would be isolated."

Richards's friend said that he did not take these grandiose remarks seriously.

The prosecution also introduced the testimony of Michael Waller, an expert from the state crime laboratory. Waller stated that microscopic examination of television cable seized in Richards's pickup truck at the time of the arrest positively matched the cable used to wrap Baldwin's body. Berberian then put before the jury a collection of bank and accounting records that showed the perilous state of Richards's finances shortly before the murder.

The prosecution's case concluded with the testimony of the security guard who had challenged Richards and his two young employees at the Loch Lomond Marina; a Mill Valley man who had sold Richards the boat on 6 July, and Richards's former wife. Caryn, who had now reassumed her family-name, Cerutti, stated that on the night of the dumping of the body in San Pablo Bay, her husband had left home at about 11:30 p.m. and had not returned until 3:00 a.m., when he had fallen into a deep sleep. She told the jury of her surprise that Richards could afford the boat or even the charm-bracelet that he had presented to her shortly after the day of the murder.

The defence attempted to challenge the prosecution's chronological reconstruction of the crime by calling a witness who swore that he had seen Richard Baldwin alive on the night of 6 July 1982. Robert Hudsmith testified that his shower-drain was plugged and that between 10 and 11 p. m. he had gone to a chimney-cleaning firm located near The Classic Car to try to borrow a "snake". At the chimney-cleaner's an assistant named Devon Hird had told Hudsmith that she did not have a snake but suggested he borrow one from Baldwin. Hudsmith did not follow her advice because he knew that the car-dealer did not lend his tools – but he clearly recalled seeing Baldwin talking to friends at his shop. Hird confirmed Hudsmith's story.

This defence testimony proved to be a three-day wonder. On Thursday, rebuttal evidence gathered by Detective Lindquist proved that Hudsmith had been mistaken as to the date. The prosecution introduced a rental agreement showing that Hudsmith had rented a plumber's "snake" in the early afternoon of 6 July and returned it half an hour later; he had visited the chimney-cleaner's and seen Baldwin a week earlier, on 29 June.

In his closing argument for the prosecution, Deputy District Attorney Berberian asserted that the defendant "lied at the beginning, in the middle and at the end, to cover up the murder of Richard Baldwin". Berberian pointed out that the load of trash that Richards and his two employees were taking to the dump at the time of their arrest included the cable and plastic sheeting linking him to the murder. Shapiro, in rejoinder, trained his major attack on Andrew's testimony, which he regarded as tainted and unworthy of belief: Andrew had implicated Mark Richards to cover his own guilt. The defence counsel also dismissed the theory of the Pendragon conspiracy:

> Mark's role-model was King Arthur. Pendragon was the dream of a young man who wanted to be King Arthur. Is that evidence of a crime? He has a creative imagination. These kids were playing a game of Knights of the Round Table and either misunderstood it or wanted it to be a game of cops and robbers or a game of war.

It took the jury four days to find Richards guilty of first-degree murder. After deliberating on the separate penalty-phase of the trial, the same jury found that the three "special circumstances" charged by the prosecution (that the murder involved a hired assassin and was motivated by financial gain and a burglary plan) were established, and Richards was sentenced to life imprisonment without possibility of parole.

After his arrest, Crossie Hoover's lawyers had argued that he should be tried as a juvenile. A child psychiatrist, Dr Roman Rodriquez, had testified that Crossie was suffering from a borderline personality disorder and that there was a "good chance" that he would not kill again if properly treated. Deputy District Attorney Berberian, finding little comfort in the odds the doctor was quoting, asked whether he was willing to bet his life on his prediction. Rodriquez could only reply that there were "no guarantees". According to the witness, Hoover was "a tool" in Richards's murder plan and, because of his mental condition and learning disability, was incapable of planning and carrying out the crime on his own. The doctor did not urge that Hoover be set free, but recommended his confinement in a mental hospital for long-term intensive treatment.

Berberian sought sterner treatment for Hoover, who had told another psychiatrist that he found killing "as easy as brushing your teeth", and advocated his trial as an adult – which, in the event of conviction, could entail a prison term of twenty-five years to life, as compared with the maximum five-year term that could be imposed on defendants prosecuted as juveniles. Juvenile Court Judge Peter Allen Smith ruled for the prosecution, finding Rodriquez's testimony too speculative and highly optimistic.

In May 1984, the legal battles in the murder case of Crossie Hoover were renewed, and the defence scored a tactical victory. After a secret hearing, granted to avoid prejudicing potential jurors, Justice Louis H. Burke ruled that Hoover's confession would not be admissible at the trial. The tape-recording of Hoover's statement revealed that San Rafael police sergeant Walt Kosta had advised the suspect of his right as a juvenile to have one of his parents present during the questioning. Hoover had answered that he wanted his mother to be called. The judge stated that at this point Kosta should have immediately stopped the questioning. Instead, the sergeant had erred by taking a "second bite of the apple": he had asked Hoover to reconfirm that he wanted his mother brought to the station before talking to the police, and Crossie, perhaps taking that comment as a challenge to his manhood, had withdrawn his request and proceeded with the interview in his mother's absence.

The Pendragon conspiracy did not figure significantly in the prosecution's presentation of its case against Hoover. Deputy District Attorney Berberian advanced the straighforward argument that Hoover was motivated by Richards's promise of money. Unable, however, to resist the opportunity to make his own contribution to the psychological portraits of Baldwin's murderers, Berberian hypothesized that Hoover saw Richards's blood-money as a means of "buying the love he never had to alleviate the frustration in his life". During the course of the five-week trial, the prosecution introduced a strong chain of evidence against Crossie that more than compensated for the suppression of the youth's confession: a college student employed by Richards during the summer of 1982 testified that Hoover had bragged about killing a man, and the defendant's fingerprints were found at the scene of the crime. In his closing argument, defence attorney Edward Torrico felt compelled to concede that his client had participated in Baldwin's murder, arguing that the young man was mentally disturbed at the time. The Marin Superior Court jury found Hoover guilty after a day's deliberations.

After rendering its verdict, the jury considered Hoover's insanity plea. Dr Rodriquez, testifying for the defence, supported Torrico's argument that Hoover had slipped into a temporary psychotic state at the time he struck the fatal blows. The prosecution countered this evidence by introducing the comments that Hoover had made to a clinical psychologist in September 1982 regarding his state of mind just before the killing:

> It was like Richards was coaching me. He would listen to what I said and push me on. When I was with Baldwin, I kept thinking, this is the guy standing between me and money. It made me excited. I thought about guns I could buy and all the other stuff. I knew it was wrong, but I didn't give a damn. Did you ever think of getting $5000? Did you ever think of wanting to be with your mother? My mother would come back to Marin County. I could have my own room so I wouldn't have to look at her all the time. Oh, man. I was just thinking of how happy I'd be, how much love I would get, how many things I'd have.

As Berberian reflected on this statement, he must have wondered which were more chilling, the imperial dreams of Mark Richards or his hireling's limited mental horizons.

The jury rejected Hoover's insanity defence, and in November 1984 he was sentenced to twenty-six years to life. In February 1987 his conviction was affirmed by a California appellate court. The board had been swept clean; the new Camelot had lost both its King and its knight.

Last Stop, Arcadia

Jonathan Goodman

ALTHOUGH THE BARROW Gang – led by Clyde Barrow, a diminutive, psychopathic, sexually indeterminate saxophone-player, the last person that anyone in *his* right mind would have bought a used getaway car from – achieved little in the way of loot from their raids on small-town banks, petrol stations, greasy-spoon transport cafés, and establishments called Piggly Wiggly Stores (their largest haul was $1500), they were responsible, between them, for at least eighteen murders.

Clyde Barrow

On 23 May 1934, a Wednesday, Barrow and his moll, Bonnie Parker, her nymphomania only whetted by their sharing of beds, rumble-seats, and dry ditches in the course of their strange odyssey over the previous four years or so, were killed in an ambush near Arcadia, Louisiana. Clyde, who was twenty-five, and who had been driving with his shoes off, had not had time to put them on; Bonnie, who was twenty-three, had not had time to swallow a mouthful of ham-sandwich that she had bitten off a moment before Clyde stamped his tartan-socked foot, probably painfully, on the brake-pedal. (Why anyone should have bothered to count the number of bullets fired into the car by the ambushing party, I have no idea, but the total was reported as 167; assuming that the counter was good at sums, and since there is no reason to suppose that the ambushers were better shots than was usually so, it is reasonable to guess that some 300 bullets were fired with the intention of striking the car or its occupants.)

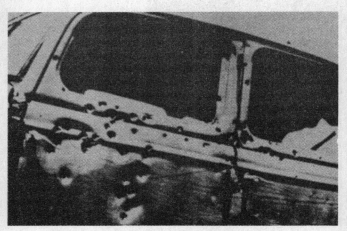

Part of the ambushed car

Bonnie Parker

Bonnie Parker has been described as "crime's answer to Elizabeth Barrett Browning"; but, as the following examples of her work show, the comparison is not strictly accurate.

The Story of Suicide Sal

We, each of us, have a good alibi
For being down here in the joint;
But few of them are really justified,
If you get right down to the point.

You have heard of a woman's glory
Being spent on a downright cur.
Still you can't always judge the story
As true being told by her.

As long as I stayed on the island
And heard confidence tales from the gals,
There was only one interesting and truthful,
It was the story of Suicide Sal.

> Now Sal was a girl of rare beauty,
> Tho' her features were somewhat tough,
> She never once faltered from duty,
> To play on the up and up.
>
> Sal told me this tale on the evening
> Before she was turned out free,
> And I'll do my best to relate it
> Just as she told it to me.
>
> I was born on a ranch in Wyoming,
> Not treated like Helen of Troy,
> Was taught that rods were rulers,
> And ranked with greasy cowboys . . .

Further verses were intended, but Bonnie was interrupted by the arrival of "a motorized posse of law enforcement officers" outside the house where she and the rest of the gang were staying. This happened at Joplin, Missouri, in April 1933. The gang escaped, leaving two policemen dead; a search of the house revealed an arsenal of rifles in an upstairs room and the unfinished poem on the dining-room table.

Towards the end of July 1933, following the killing of Buck Barrow, Clyde's elder brother, and the capture of Buck's wife Blanche (a preacher's daughter who put her fingers in her ears during gunfights), Bonnie composed her masterpiece, "The Story of Bonnie and Clyde", and sent it to a Dallas newspaper, requesting publication after her death:

> You've heard the story of Jesse James –
> Of how he lived and died.
> If you're still in need
> Of something to read,
> Here's the story of Bonnie and Clyde.
>
> Now Bonnie and Clyde are the Barrow Gang.
> I'm sure you all have read
> How they rob and steal
> And those who squeal
> Are usually found dying or dead.
>
> They call them cold-hearted killers;
> They say they are heartless and mean;
> But I say this with pride,
> That I once knew Clyde
> When he was honest and upright and clean.

Bonnie & Clyde

But the laws fooled around,
Kept taking him down
And locking him up in a cell,
Till he said to me,
I'll never be free,
So I'll meet a few of them in hell!

The road was so dimly lighted;
There were no highway signs to guide;
But they made up their minds,
If all roads were blind,
They wouldn't give up till they died.

The road gets dimmer and dimmer;
Sometimes you can hardly see;
But it's fight man to man,
And do all you can,
For they know they can never be free.

If they try to act like citizens,
And rent them a nice little flat,
About the third night
They're invited to fight
By a submachine-gun rat-tat-tat.

They don't think they are too tough or desperate,
They know the law always wins,
They have been shot at before
But they do not ignore
That death is the wages of sin.

From heartbreaks some people have suffered,
From weariness some people have died,
But take it all in all,
Our troubles are small,
Till we get like Bonnie and Clyde.

Some day they will go down together,
And they will bury them side by side,
To a few it means grief,
To the law it's relief,
But it's death to Bonnie and Clyde.

Bonnie and Clyde were not buried side by side. His colander-like remains were interred next to his brother Buck's less punctured ones in a cemetery at Dallas, in their home-state of Texas. Bonnie's laying to rest was in two instalments: her first burial (at which a quartet sang "Beautiful Isle of Somewhere") was in the Fish Trap Cemetery, not far from her place of birth, Rowena, also in Texas; her second – organized, it seems, because someone had tardily decided that Fish Trap was too unromantic-sounding a place for the end of the legend that was already being concocted – was in the Crown Hill Memorial Park. If only as an example of the notorious inaccuracy of epitaphs, it is worth quoting the lines inscribed on the headstone above one of Bonnie Parker's graves:

> As the flowers are all made sweeter
> By the sunshine and the dew,
> So this old world is made brighter
> By the lives of folks like you[3].

---

3. Equally inappropriate words were inscribed on the gravestone of Belle Starr (1848–89), the American outlaw known as "the petticoat of the plains", whose crimes included horse-theft, murder and torture for gain. Her epitaph is said to have been composed by her illegitimate daughter Pearl:

> Shed not for her the bitter tear
> Nor give the heart to vain regret;
> 'Tis but the casket that lies here,
> The gem that fills it sparkles yet.

Acknowledgements and Sources

"The Four-Wheeled Crematorium", a version of a series that appeared in the *Manchester Evening News*, is published by permission of the author; "Fire-lit Tales of Murder" is published by permission of the author; "The Judge's Black Cadillac" is published by permission of the author; "Woman of Evil", a chapter in *Squad Man* (London, 1973), appears by courtesy of that book's publishers, W. H. Allen & Co plc; "Looking for Baby-Face" is published by permission of the author; "The Hit-and-Run Murderer", an extract from *Court of Murder: Famous Trials at Glasgow High Court* (John Long, London, 1968), is published by permission of the author; "The Hansom Hearse" is an extract from *Memories of Famous Trials* (Sisley's, London, 1907); "The Wicked Hansom" is a chapter from *More Studies in Murder* (Smith & Haas, New York, 1936); "The Case of the Equivocal Cabbie" is made up of extracts from the Introduction to *The Trial of Alexander Campbell Mason* (Geoffrey Bles, London, 1930); "Nemesis in Texas" is a chapter from *Crimes of the Year* (Allen & Unwin, London, 1932); "Killed After a Cuddle", a chapter from *The Trials of Mr Justice Avory* (Rich & Cowan, London, 1935), is published by permission of the author's son, Peter O'Donnell; "A Murder in Camelot" is published by permission of the author; "Last Stop, Arcadia", a version of an entry in *Bloody Versicles: The Rhymes of Crime* (David & Charles, Newton Abbot, 1971), is published by permission of the author.